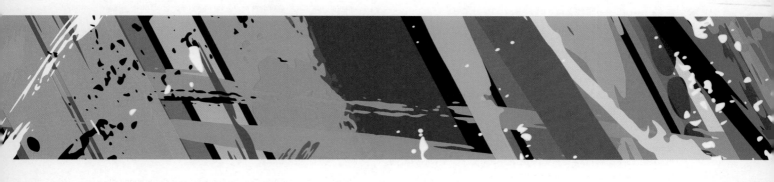

Getting **Familiar** with the**Unfamiliar** 1

Understanding Unfamiliar Text Through Close Reading: NCEA Level One

Kathryn **Fitzgerald** and **Tania** Roxborogh

NELSON
A Cengage Company

Getting Familiar with the Unfamiliar
1st Edition
Kathryn Fitzgerald
Tania Roxborogh

Cover designer: Cheryl Smith
Text designer: Cheryl Smith
Production controller: Siew Han Ong

Any URLs contained in this publication were checked for currency during the production process. Note, however, that the publisher cannot vouch for the ongoing currency of URLs.

Acknowledgements
The authors and publisher wish to thank the following people and organisations for permission to use the resources in this textbook.
Page 9, *Friendly Persuasion from Short Stories from New Zealand* selected by Alan Paterson, courtesy of David Hill and Highgate/Price Milburn Ltd; page 18, *Four Letters of Love* by Niall Williams courtesy of Picador; page 24, *The Crimson Petal and the White* by Michael Faber courtesy of Canongate Books; page 30, *Red Pen* courtesy of Audrey Philips; page 34, *Third Degree* courtesy of Tania Roxborogh and Longacre Press; page 36, Beach Patrol from *Charlie Tangaroa and the Creature from the Sea* courtesy of T.K Roxborogh; page 40, *My Sister's Top* courtesy of Ruth Sun; page 47, *Invigilator* by Janet Charmen courtesy of Auckland University Press; page 54, *Tooth* courtesy of Siobhan Harvey; page 55, *If We Return* courtesy of F.W. Harvey; page 64, *Morning* from *Picnic, Lighting* by Billy Collins courtesy of Pittsburgh Press; page 66, *A Work of Artifice* courtesy of Marge Piercy; page 70, *At Ten Years Old* courtesy of Catlin Addison; page 76, *Head Boy's Prizegiving Speech* courtesy of Jakob Bailey; page 83, *A World of Books* courtesy of T.K. Roxborogh; page 89, *The Rude Question* courtesy of Frania Cowie; page 92, *Ducks and Drakes* courtesy of Kelvin Wright; page 94, *Teenagers, or Seeds?* courtesy of Elin Harris.

© 2017 Cengage Learning Australia Pty Limited

For product information and technology assistance,
in Australia call **1300 790 853**;
in New Zealand call **0800 449 725**

For permission to use material from this text or product, please email
aust.permissions@cengage.com

National Library of New Zealand Cataloguing-in-Publication Data
A catalogue record for this book is available from the National Library of New Zealand

978 0 17 041596 5

Cengage Learning Australia
Level 7, 80 Dorcas Street
South Melbourne, Victoria Australia 3205

Cengage Learning New Zealand
Unit 4B Rosedale Office Park
331 Rosedale Road, Albany, North Shore 0632, NZ

For learning solutions, visit **cengage.co.nz**

Printed in China by 1010 Printing International Limited
11 12 25 24

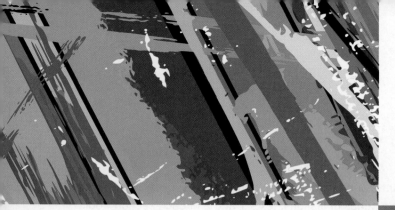

Contents

> The terms 'features' and 'techniques' are used interchangeably in this book.

 When you see this icon, we want you to use at least one 'because' in your answer. The word 'because' is a magic word, as it forces you to explain and justify your statements.

 When you see this icon, it means it is a term you might be unsure of, so we have included a definition in the glossary.

INTRODUCTION FOR TEACHERS

We have created this workbook for students to use with little or no teacher intervention, however, it would also be a great resource in the classroom. For example, taken as a series of lessons, texts 1 and 2 of each section would take two to three hours *each* to work through thoroughly as a class. Hopefully, you can see the benefit in breaking down the texts like this, and you are welcome to use this structure as a blueprint to create your own resources for unfamiliar texts. The book is designed to be used either from start to finish or as fits the needs of your students.

Recommended reading
Teaching Reading Comprehension Strategies by Sheena Cameron. This is a practical classroom guide that will expand on some of the techniques we use in this workbook.

INTRODUCTION FOR STUDENTS

Congratulations! By opening this book you have taken a big step in improving your understanding of unfamiliar texts. The term 'unfamiliar text' in an exam refers to a text that you are unlikely to have come across before. This may seem daunting, but, in fact, you read unfamiliar texts every day: the articles that people share on Facebook, a text message from a friend, the advert on the back of a bus — you understand these, don't you? The exam is just a more formal version of what you are doing every single day. The key is to realise that all texts follow a similar pattern and that you actually already have many of the tools you need to get familiar with the unfamiliar.

The aim of this book is to help you recognise patterns in a text and to access and practise using reading tools so that you will feel calm and confident going into the end-of-year exam.

In each section, the first text will have lots of activities that will help you understand the three key parts to answering the exam questions well:

1 What do the words **say**? (definition of the words)
2 What do the words **mean**? (interpretation of the words)
3 **Why** have the words been used? (purpose or author's intent)

As you work through each section, you will be able to recognise patterns and the activities will slowly be withdrawn until finally, at the end of each section, there are two texts that are presented in a similar way to those in the exam.

One of the most daunting things in the unfamiliar text exam is that sometimes you don't understand some, or many, of the words that are in the text and in the question. Because of this, the first activity for each text is always a vocabulary one. We can't guarantee that any of these words will be in the exam, but we are hoping that these activities will help to expand your own vocabulary. We have been able to include only a small variety of ways to work with words you don't know and it is important that you realise there are other options. These will be things that you do most days without realising.

ISBN: 9780170415965

There are *seven key strategies* to help you approach words you don't know and they are:

1 Reread.
2 Read on.
3 Break down the word.
4 Use what you've already read to guess the meaning.
5 Use pictures, graphs, caption boxes, and/or photos around the text to look for clues.
6 Ask someone.
7 Check a dictionary.

It is good to be aware that there are deliberate strategies you can use to help you understand what you are reading, but obviously numbers 6 and 7 will not be available in the exam.

Let us show you how some of these strategies can be used.

The **kea** (/ˈkiː.ə/; Māori: [kɛ.a]; Nestor notabilis) is a large species of parrot of the family Strigopidae found in forested and alpine regions of the South Island of New Zealand. About 48 cm (19 in) long, it is mostly olive-green with a brilliant orange under its wings and has a large, narrow, curved, grey-brown upper beak. The kea is the world's only alpine parrot. Its omnivorous diet includes carrion,[2] but consists mainly of roots, leaves, berries, nectar, and insects. Now uncommon, the kea was once killed for bounty due to concerns by the sheep-farming community that it attacked livestock, especially sheep.

Source: https://en.wikipedia.org/wiki/Kea

	Words I am unsure of	Strategy I used	How the strategy helped
1	Strigopidae	Reread	When I reread this sentence, I saw that it says the kea is a large species of parrot in the family Strigopidae. I can infer (deduce/ guess) that this is the formal, scientific name for that type of bird.
2	alpine	Read on Reread	I see that alpine is mentioned again. When that still doesn't help, I go back and *reread*. I see that alpine is connected with the word forested and the South Island, so I can guess that it is a way to describe the physical area where the kea live. I know the South Island has a high mountain range, so I can guess that this is what it means.
3	omnivorous	Read on	This sentence includes a list of what the kea eat. It has a variety of things so I can tell that omnivorous means meat (insects) and fruit (berries).
4	carrion	Ask someone	There are no clues as to what carrion means when I reread and read on, so I ask a friend what it means. It means the rotting flesh of dead animals. Ewww.
5	bounty	Use a dictionary	There are also no clues as to what this means, and my friend doesn't know, so I grab my device and google 'bounty'. It means a reward for killing an animal.

Now you have a turn:

Read the following paragraph and use at least one of the strategies at the top of the previous page to figure out what the words mean. Try to use **reread**, **read on** or **break down the word**, as you won't be able to ask a friend or use a dictionary in the exam!

Lava *is the molten rock expelled by a volcano during an eruption. The resulting rock after solidification and cooling is also called lava. The molten rock is formed in the interior of some planets, including Earth, and some of their satellites. The source of the heat that melts the rock within the earth is geothermal energy. When first erupted from a volcanic vent, lava is a liquid usually at temperatures from 700 to 1200°C (1292 to 2192°F).*

Source: https://en.wikipedia.org/wiki/Lava

	Words I am unsure of	Strategy I used	How the strategy helped
1	molten		
2	expelled		
3	solidification		
4	geothermal		
5	vent		
6			

Now that you have learned about the seven deliberate reading strategies, try them out in your daily reading. When you see something you don't understand, work through it using one or more of the strategies.

Completing this workbook will increase your chances of doing well in the unfamiliar text exam but don't underestimate the usefulness of reading something new every single day. The exam will cover narrative prose (fiction), poetry and non-fiction, so make sure you cover all of these categories regularly in your reading.

We have designed this book so that you can either work through from start to finish or choose one of the sections that appeals to you and start there.

Good luck!

ISBN: 9780170415965

SectionOne: NARRATIVE PROSE

NARRATIVE PROSE 1

Narrative prose, also known commonly as fiction, is probably the type of writing you are most familiar with, as you would have had stories read to you before you were even aware of what the written word was. Stories are always made for a purpose: to entertain, to inform, to persuade, to empathise, to teach ... The list is endless. The key is for you to recognise what the purpose is for the text you are reading.

Pre-reading activities

*Before you read the short story, let's prepare by looking at some words that might be new to you. Next, we will consider any ideas you may already have about other words. Finally, we will look at ways to 'predict' the subject and **tone** of the extract from these words.*

> **G**
>
> **Tone**: the overall impression of the author's attitude towards the topic or a character or event. For example: humorous, sad, formal, light-hearted, sarcastic, serious.

1 VOCABULARY WORK

Write a full sentence that includes the specified word. If you are unsure of the meaning of any of the words, look them up.

a inherited *I **inherited** my grandmother's engagement ring.*
_____

b expelled _____
_____

c persuaded _____
_____

d transferred _____
_____

e atmosphere _____
_____

f armament _____
_____

g pouting _____
_____

h apprentice(s) _____
_____

i Cavalier _____
_____

j holy orders _____
_____

ISBN: 9780170415965

2 THE TITLE

The title of a text tells us a lot about the subject matter and/or the author's purpose. It is worth spending a bit of time working out what the title might mean. The first text is from a short story called 'Friendly Persuasion' by David Hill.

a In the spaces below, write down the literal (dictionary) definition of the word and then, beside it, what ideas or feelings the word suggests to you. (These 'suggestions' are called **connotations**.)

Friendly _____ _____

_____ _____

Persuasion _____ _____

_____ _____

b Look at the definitions of the vocab from **1** on the previous page, and finish this sentence:

I think the story might be about _____

_____

because _____

_____

_____

_____

_____ .

> **The magic 'because'**
> The word 'because' is a magic word as it forces us to explain and justify our statements.

3 THE BACKGROUND/CONTEXT OF THE EXTRACT

When you read a text, it is important that you take into consideration all the available information: who the author is (male, female, non-binary, transgender, age, nationality, occupation, religion, politics, and so on), when the text was written, where the text is based, and any other details provided, as this can go some way to assisting you in understanding the purpose of the text.

In the exam, this information is usually provided within the question, and in the small print under the text.

This story first appeared in an anthology called *Short Stories from New Zealand* (1988). The version here is abridged. Before he was a writer, David Hill was a secondary school English teacher. The intended audience is secondary school students.

> **Abridged:** (of a book, film, poem) shortened without losing the main sense of it.

Write down three to six words that you would associate with the word 'school'.

_____ _____ _____

_____ _____ _____

ISBN: 9780170415965

Reading the text

1 Read the extract through once, slowly (out loud if you can). Don't do anything else; just read.

Friendly Persuasion

The school inherited Alan after he left the neighbouring Boys' High. His reasons for leaving were never made entirely clear. As far as could be discovered, he hadn't actually been expelled, but his parents had been persuaded that it might be in everybody's best interests if Alan transferred his particular talents elsewhere. Alan's parents were easily persuaded into most things; they found it a lot less trouble than having to make their own decisions.

Slim, tanned, black-haired and hazel-eyed, Alan was totally charming and totally irresponsible. Alan was never an actual discipline problem in class. He naturally didn't intend to do any work himself, but he had no objection to others getting on with it. Unfortunately, his effect upon those others was disastrous. The girls all wanted to mother him; the boys all wanted to smother him. By the time he'd been in any class for a week, the atmosphere was fairly crackling.

In the third week, there was an incident in Biology straight out of *Days of Our Lives*. Alan had spent Tuesday whispering to a giggly little redhead. On Wednesday he turned his armament on the pouting blonde just behind him. Thirty minutes into the Biology lesson, blonde and redhead were suddenly locked in mortal combat. Alan's parents were invited along to the Principal's study.

Alan's parents sat with the Principal for half an hour, looked anxious, wanted to help, but didn't know what to do. What would the Principal suggest? Alan was such a cheerful boy at home that they didn't want to upset him. If any of the teachers had suggestions, they'd be happy to listen. Did the Principal know that they'd just bought Alan a second-hand Mini as a birthday present? Perhaps that would help keep him out of trouble.

Alan's Mini was suddenly the focus of the school's attention. By this time, he'd gathered a small following of apprentice Romeos, and they spent most of their lunchtimes draped across the Mini's bonnet holding court to queues of wistful Year 10 and 11 Juliets. Alan at this stage sported a long scarf in school colours that a blushing little net-baller had knitted for him. Tossed casually around his neck, it made him look like a Cavalier on holiday. His apprentices hastily acquired similar scarves. Around their necks, the stripes made them look like a chorus of bullfrogs. The Principal did know about Alan's Mini.

The first call was from a mother whose pre-schooler had almost been demolished by a speeding car full of high school children. Yes, she was sure they were from the high school; she'd seen the scarves they were wearing. The second call was from a furious pensioner whose front lawn now displayed two skid marks from a white Mini that had just done wheelies across it. The third was from the local Police Station. They had a Y11 girl whom they'd found being very sick at the side of the road. Smelt like a lounge bar, she did. There'd been a carload of them, apparently, but the others had driven off before the police arrived.

Alan, when he received the summons to the Principal's study, was misguided enough to try another friendly smile. Alan was given 10 minutes to clear out his locker. He and his Mini were pointed in the direction of the front gate, and the Principal began the necessary phone calls. The staff sighed in relief. The Y11 girls, when the news reached them, went pale and threatened to take holy orders.

A week later the school was back to normal. Classroom life became placid again and the Year 11 girls found other idols. The staff started to feel a bit more charitable. After all, they'd known characters like Alan before. Proper ratbags at school, but usually they straightened themselves out when they left. Became responsible and mature, as they did in all the best stories.

Life in this case was more ruthless than fiction. Only a month after his departure, Alan's Mini left the highway on an S-bend, somersaulted down a bank and caught fire. Alan was supposed to be grounded at home, but he'd managed to persuade his parents that he was repentant enough to be allowed a night out. By the time rescue crews extinguished the flames, Alan and his Mini were unrecognisable.

From 'Friendly Persuasion' by David Hill. First published in *Short Stories from New Zealand*, selected by Alistair Paterson, 1988, Highgate/Price Milburn Ltd, Petone.

ISBN: 9780170415965

2 Now that you have read through the text, finish the following sentence:

My first impression of this extract is _____

_____

because _____

_____.

3 Read the extract through again. Look at your predictions from the prereading activities — were you correct? Complete the following statements:

I was correct when I predicted _____

_____.

I was incorrect when I predicted _____

_____.

I think this is because _____

_____

_____

_____

_____.

One thing that surprised me about the story was _____

_____

_____.

4 Who do you think is the intended audience: students, parents, and/or teachers?

_____

Give evidence from the text to support your answer.

_____

_____

_____

_____

_____

ISBN: 9780170415965

Using the 'Three Level Reading Guide'

This guide will help you to gain a deeper understanding of the text, starting with the basics and going towards a deeper analysis of the text.

Level One: **Literal** meanings or 'on the surface' statements. The information can easily be found in the text.

Level Two: **Interpretation** of the Level One statements, or 'between the lines'. You say what you think the writer means using your understanding of the information provided.

Level Three: **Application** of the ideas by 'going beyond the lines'. You make judgements based on the information in the text and your own interpretations.

1 Read each statement below and circle whether it is **TRUE** or **FALSE**. (Thinking about these statements will help you gain a deeper understanding of the text.)

Level One: **Literal** meanings or 'on the surface' statements.

a	Alan is the narrator.	TRUE/FALSE
b	Alan used to attend Boys' High.	TRUE/FALSE
c	Alan is attractive.	TRUE/FALSE
d	Alan had been expelled.	TRUE/FALSE

Level Two: **Interpretation** of the Level One statements or 'between the lines'.

a	The narrator finds Alan amusing.	TRUE/FALSE
b	Alan is lazy and not intelligent.	TRUE/FALSE
c	Alan's parents are good parents.	TRUE/FALSE
d	The school did not want Alan.	TRUE/FALSE

Level Three: **Application** of the ideas by 'going beyond the lines'.

a	People were upset by Alan's behaviour.	TRUE/FALSE
b	The narrator understands teenagers.	TRUE/FALSE
c	People who want to have fun in life are bad people.	TRUE/FALSE
d	Alan's parents have failed to teach him the right way to live.	TRUE/FALSE

2 Choose one of the Level Three statements (going beyond the lines) that you believe is true and explain why you think it is true. Use evidence from the text to support your answer.

Letter: _____

This is true because _____

_____

_____

_____.

Remember that 'because' is magic.

Identifying the 'point of change'

G

*All fiction (narrative prose) has a 'point of change' in it. The point of change shows us the narrator's **attitude** to the subject, which helps understand the author's purpose. Identifying and understanding the point of change is key to your receiving a good grade for your answer.*

1 Read the story again. You will see that the start of each paragraph is indicated by an indent. Identify which paragraph we start to see a point of change. _____

2 Briefly describe the change._____

_____

3 How does this point of change help us understand the purpose of this piece of writing?

_____

_____

_____

Using the title to help you understand the author's purpose

1 Why do you think the title of this story is appropriate?

_____

_____

2 How does this relate to the author's attitude towards the characters in his story?

_____

_____

3 Write a different title for the story and explain why you chose this title.

_____

_____

_____

_____

4 How do the title and the point of change work together to get the author's purpose across to the reader?

_____

_____

_____

_____

_____

ISBN: 9780170415965

Identifying how the text is communicated

*The choice of words and phrases helps communicate the author's attitude to what they are writing about. Identifying the **tone** of a passage will help you understand the author's purpose in writing the text. Ideas are communicated through a variety of **language features or language techniques**. These terms are used interchangeably in this book. In the box below, we have identified many of the features used in the story.*

1 The following **language features** can be found in the text. Find and label on the text (on page 9) an example of each of the techniques in the box below. Refer to the glossary (at the back of the book) if you do not know these words.

repetition	adjective	adverb	metaphor
compound word	parallel construction	onomatopoeia	question
listing	simile	alliteration	euphemism

2 Identify one metaphor in the text and describe its significance.

_____

_____

_____

3 The author uses a lot of euphemism (when you use mild or inoffensive words or phrases instead of harsh or blunt ones, for example 'kicked the bucket' instead of 'died'). Find two examples and explain what the more direct meaning is.

Example One:

_____

_____

Example Two:

_____

_____

Putting it all together

Now that you have spent some time 'unpacking' the extract, recognising its language features, and thought about the effects, the meaning and the author's purpose, it's time to put all the parts together again and practise writing the types of answers you will need to write in your examination. You can use the notes you have made in the previous pages to help you.

1 Select (✓) ONE language feature from paragraphs two to four that the writer uses to describe Alan.

☐ adjective ☐ metaphor ☐ alliteration
☐ listing ☐ repetition ☐ compound word
☐ question ☐ euphemism ☐ contrast

2 Give an example of this language feature from paragraphs two to four.

_____

_____

3 Explain how this and/or other language feature(s) help you to **understand** the narrator's **attitude towards Alan**. You could refer back to your responses on the previous pages to help you with your answer. You might consider:

• the effect Alan has on his parents
• the effect Alan has on the other students and the teachers
• the key message(s) the narrator wanted the reader to understand.

We have included starter sentences for your paragraph. Complete each sentence thoroughly and you will have a great paragraph answer.

The author, David Hill, wanted to highlight the issue of _____

because _____

_____.

He does this by using the technique of _____ when he writes

[insert quote] '_____,'

This is effective because _____

_____.

Another technique the author uses is _____, for example when

he says [insert different quote] '_____,'

This means _____

_____

and is used to emphasis the idea that _____

_____

This makes us think about _____

_____ so that we do/do not

_____

_____

_____.

ISBN: 9780170415965

Finally, the author wanted us to remember/act/learn that _____

_____

because _____

_____

_____

just like in the story when _____

_____

_____

_____.

NARRATIVE PROSE 2

Pre-reading activities

Before you read the extract, let's prepare by looking at some words that might be new to you. Next, we will consider any ideas you may already have about other words. Finally, we will look at ways to 'predict' the subject and **tone** *of the extract from these words.*

G

Tone: the overall impression of the author's attitude towards the topic, or a character or event. For example: humorous, sad, formal, light-hearted, sarcastic, serious.

1 VOCABULARY WORK

Look up the following words and write the most common meaning beside each.

a civil servant _____
(you may need to look these two up separately)

_____

b severity _____

_____

c wiry _____

_____

d angular _____

_____

e fewness _____

_____

f frailty _____

_____

g emerges _____

_____

Write down 3-6 words that you would associate with the word 'father'.

_____   _____   _____

_____   _____   _____

Write down 3-6 words that you would associate with the word 'God'.

_____   _____   _____

_____   _____   _____

ISBN: 9780170415965   PHOTOCOPYING OF THIS PAGE IS RESTRICTED UNDER LAW.

2 THE TITLE

Remember that the title of a text tells us a lot about the subject matter and/or the author's purpose. This extract is from a novel called *Four Letters of Love* by Niall Williams.

In the spaces below, write down the **literal** (dictionary) definition of the word and then, beside it, what ideas or feelings the word suggests to you. (These 'suggestions' are called **connotations**.)

Four *A cardinal number* _____ *There is more than one of something.* _____

Letters _____ _____

Of _____ _____

Love _____ _____

Look at the definitions of the vocabulary from **1** above, and finish this sentence:

I think the novel might be about _____

because _____

_____.

3 THE BACKGROUND/CONTEXT OF THE EXTRACT

When you read a text, it is important that you take into consideration all the available information: who the author is (male, female, non-binary, transgender, age, nationality, occupation, religion, politics, and so on), when the text was written, where the text is based, and any other details provided, as this can go some way to assisting you in understanding the purpose of the text.

In the exam, this information is usually provided within the question, and in the small print under the text.

This book is based in Ireland and was written in 1997. The author is male and was born in Dublin in 1958. Write down three to six words that you would associate with the word 'Ireland' or 'Irish'.

_____ _____ _____

_____ _____ _____

The extract mentions the place Greystones. Find out about this place. Write down three things about this town. An example could be: It is a town in the northern hemisphere.

a _____

b _____

c _____

Reading the text

1 Read this opening paragraph of *Four Letters of Love* once, slowly (out loud if you can). Don't do anything else; just read.

> *When I was twelve years old God spoke to my father for the first time. God didn't say much.*
> *He told my father to be a painter, and left it at that, returning to a seat amongst the angels*
> *and watching through the clouds over the grey city to see what would happen next.*

2 What information about the narrator, tone and topic of the text do we gain from this opening?

a The narrator is _____

_____

b The tone is _____

_____

c The text is going to be about _____

_____

3 Read the text through once, without doing anything else; just read it through slowly.
Remember, this story is set in the northern hemisphere where the seasons are opposite to New Zealand's. So, when the extract mentions 'the fog of November', it is autumn.

Four Letters of Love

When I was twelve years old God spoke to my father for the first time. God didn't say much. He told my father to be a painter, and left it at that, returning to a seat amongst the angels and watching through the clouds over the grey city to see what would happen next.

At the time my father was a civil servant. He was a thin man, tall and wiry, with bones poking out into his skin. His hair had turned silver when he was twenty-four and given him a look of age and severity which was later to deepen and increase to such an extent that he could not walk down a street without catching notice. He looked touched by something, an impression furthered by the dazzling blueness of his eyes and the fewness of his words. Although I had no brothers or sisters, from the first twelve years of my life I can remember little of what he ever said to me. The words have vanished and I am left mostly with pictures of my early childhood: my father in a grey suit coming in the front door from the office in the fog of November evenings, the briefcase flopping by the telephone table, the creak in the stairs and across the ceiling above the kitchen as he changes into a cardigan and comes down for his tea. The great shelf of his forehead floating up above the line of a newspaper in the response to some question. The New Year's Day swims in the frozen sea at Greystones. I hold his towel and he walks his high frailty into the water, his ribcage and shoulders like a twisted jumble of coat hangers in an empty suit bag. His toes curve up off the stones, off the ends of his arms he seems to carry invisible bags. Seagulls don't move from him and the pale gleam of his naked body as he stands before the blue-grey sea might be the colour of the wind. My father is thin as air, when a high wave crashes across his wading things it might snap him like a wafer. I think the sea will wash him away, but it never does. He emerges and takes the towel. For a moment he stands without drying. I am hooded and zippered into my coat and feel the wind that is freezing him. Still, he stands and looks out in the grey bay, waiting that moment before dressing himself into the New Year, not yet knowing that God is about to speak.

He had always painted. On summer evenings after the grass was cut, he might sit at the end of the garden with a sketchpad and pencils, drawing and cleaning lines as the light dies and boys kicked a ball down the street. As an eight-year-old boy with freckles and poor eye, I would look down from my bedroom window before crawling under the blankets, and feel in that still, angular figure at the end of the garden something as pure, peaceful, and good as a night-time prayer. My mother would bring him tea. She admired his talent then, and although none of his pictures ever decorated the walls of our little house, they were frequently gifts to relations and neighbours. I had heard him praised, and noted with a boy's pride the small WC that was his mark in the corner of the pictures, pushing my train along the carpet, driven with the secret knowledge that there was no one with a dad like mine.

From *Four Letters of Love* by Niall Williams, published by Picador, 1997.

This extract focuses on the narrator describing his father.

4 a Use the space below to **draw** your first impressions of the father. Leave space around your drawing.

b Now you have drawn the father, label parts of the picture with quotes to match what you have drawn. For example, a large forehead — 'The great shelf of his forehead floating …'.

c For each quote that you have written, identify the language technique that Williams has used.
Example: large forehead — 'The great shelf of his forehead floating …' — metaphor.

5 Why do you think the narrator focuses on a physical description of his father? Compare it to how you would describe your father to someone. What is missing?

_____

_____

 6 What can we **infer** (hint; imply; suggest) about the relationship between the narrator and his father from his focus on physical description?

_____

_____

7 Read the extract through again. Look at your predictions from the prereading activities — were you correct? Complete the following statements:

a I was correct when I predicted _____.

b I was incorrect when I predicted _____

I think this is because _____

_____

c One thing that surprised me about the poem was _____

_____

Using the 'Three Level Reading Guide'

This guide will help you to gain a deeper understanding of the text, starting with the basics and going towards a deeper analysis of the text.

1 Read each statement below and circle whether it is true or false. (Thinking about these statements will help you gain a deeper understanding of the text.)

Level One: **Literal** meanings or 'on the surface' statements. The information can easily be found in the text.	Level Two: **Interpretation** of the Level One statements, or 'between the lines'. You say what you think the writer means using your understanding of the information provided.	Level Three: **Application** of the ideas by 'going beyond the lines'. You make judgements based on the information in the text and your own interpretations.

Level One: **Literal** meanings or 'on the surface' statements.

a	The narrator is a boy.	TRUE/FALSE
b	The father is a talkative man.	TRUE/FALSE
c	The narrator is an only child.	TRUE/FALSE
d	The father is overweight.	TRUE/FALSE

ISBN: 9780170415965   PHOTOCOPYING OF THIS PAGE IS RESTRICTED UNDER LAW.

Level Two: **Interpretation** of the Level One statements, or 'between the lines'.

a	The narrator is older now.	TRUE/FALSE
b	God spoke to the father more than once.	TRUE/FALSE
c	The father is fit and active.	TRUE/FALSE
d	The narrator is religious.	TRUE/FALSE

Level Three: **Application** of the ideas by 'going beyond the lines'.

a	The father is spontaneous and carefree.	TRUE/FALSE
b	The narrator is no longer proud of his father's painting ability.	TRUE/FALSE
c	The father is weighed down with responsibility.	TRUE/FALSE
d	The father and mother are no longer together.	TRUE/FALSE

2 For one of the 'going beyond the lines' statements that is true, explain why you think it is true. Use evidence from the passage to back up your answer.

_____

_____

_____

_____

_____

Identifying the 'point of change'

Remember that the 'point of change' is key to unlocking the author's purpose.

1 Read the extract again. You will see that the start of each paragraph is indicated by an indent. Identify which

paragraph we start to see a point of change. _____

2 What is the reason for the change? Give specific examples from the text to support your point.

_____

_____

_____

_____

_____

_____

Identifying how the text is communicated

*The choice of words and phrases helps communicate the author's attitude to what they are writing about. Identifying the **tone** of a passage will help you understand the author's purpose in writing the text. Ideas are communicated through a variety of **language features or language techniques**. These terms are used interchangeably in this book. In the box below, we have identified many of the features used in the story.*

1 The following **language features** can be found in the text. Find and label on the text (on page 18) an example of each of the techniques in the box below.

repetition	adjective	adverb	metaphor
listing	simile	alliteration	compound word

2 Find one example of a simile and describe the effect.

_____

_____

3 Identify another simile and explain why it is an effective image.

_____

_____

_____

4 The author uses a lot of metaphors. Find two examples and explain the effect of each.

_____

_____

_____

_____

_____

Putting it all together

Now that you have spent some time 'unpacking' the extract, recognising its language features, and thought about the effects, the meaning and the author's purpose, it's time to put all the parts together and practise writing the types of answers you will need to write in your examination. You can use the notes you have made in the previous pages to help you.

1 Select (✓) ONE language feature from paragraph two (on page 18) to describe the father.

☐ adjective	☐ metaphor	☐ alliteration
☐ listing	☐ repetition	☐ compound word
☐ simile	☐ personification	☐ assonance

ISBN: 9780170415965

2 Give an example of this language feature.

_____

_____

_____

3 Explain how this and/or other language feature(s) help you to **understand** the narrator's **attitude towards his father**. You could refer back to your responses on the previous pages to help you with your answer. You might consider:
- what the narrator remembers as a child
- the narrator's feelings towards his father
- the words the writer chooses to create this picture of the father.

We have included starter sentences for your paragraph. Complete each sentence thoroughly and you will have a great paragraph answer.

The narrator describes his father as someone who _____

_____ .

We see this description when Williams uses the technique of _____ when he writes

[insert quote] ' _____

_____ ,

_____ .

The effect of this is to emphasise/highlight _____

_____ .

The reason for this is because _____

_____

_____ .

Another way this attitude toward his father is shown is through the way his appearance is described using the

technique of _____ , which we see in the text where it says [insert different quote]

' _____ ,

_____ .

From this we learn _____

_____

_____ .

It makes us think about _____

_____

because _____

_____

_____ .

Finally, the author wanted us to remember/act/learn/realise that _____

_____

_____

_____

NARRATIVE PROSE 3

Now that you have worked through two narrative prose (fiction) texts, we will be starting to remove some of the activities. This doesn't mean that they are no longer important, but, rather, we are hoping that you are starting to work through them naturally yourself as you read the text. Remember to pay attention to the language used, the title and your first impressions.

Reading the text

This is the opening to the novel *The Crimson Petal and the White* written by Michael Faber. It is set in Victorian England and this section introduces the setting to us through direct address. Unusually, in this case, the narrator is the book.

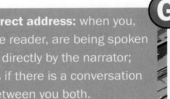

Direct address: when you, the reader, are being spoken to directly by the narrator; as if there is a conversation between you both.

1 Read the extract through once, slowly (out loud if you can). Don't do anything else; just read.

The Crimson Petal and the White

Watch your step. Keep your wits about you; you will need them. This city I am bringing you to is vast and intricate, and you have not been here before. You may imagine, from other stories you've read, that you know it well, but those stories flattered you, welcoming you as a friend, treating you as if you belonged. The truth is that you are an alien from another time and place altogether.

When I first caught your eye and you decided to come with me, you were probably thinking you would simply arrive and make yourself at home. Now that you're actually here, the air is bitterly cold, and you find yourself being led along in complete darkness, stumbling on uneven ground, recognising nothing. Looking left and right, blinking against an icy wind, you realise you have entered an unknown street of unlit houses full of unknown people.

And yet you did not choose me blindly. Certain expectations were aroused. Let's not be coy; you were hoping I would satisfy all the desires you're too shy to name, or at least show you a good time. Now you hesitate, still holding on to me, but tempted to let me go. When you first picked me up, you didn't fully appreciate the size of me, nor did you expect I would grip you so tightly, so fast. Sleet stings your cheeks, sharp little spits of it so cold they feel hot, like fiery cinders in the wind. Your ears begin to hurt. But you've allowed yourself to be led astray, and it's too late to turn back now.

It's an ashen hour of night, blacking-grey and almost readable like undisturbed pages of burnt manuscript. You blunder forward into the haze of your own spent breath, still following me. The cobblestones beneath your feet are wet and mucky, the air is frigid and smells of sour spirits and slowly dissolving dung. You hear muffled drunken voices from somewhere nearby, but what little you can understand doesn't sound like the carefully chosen opening speeches of a grand romantic drama; instead, you find yourself hoping to God that the voices come no closer.

The main characters in this story, with whom you want to become intimate, are nowhere near here. They aren't expecting you; you mean nothing to them. If you think they're going to get out of their warm beds and travel miles to meet you, you are mistaken.

You may wonder, then; why did I bring you here? Why this delay in meeting the people you thought you were going to meet? The answer is simple; their servants wouldn't have let you in the door.

What you lack is the right connections, and that is what I've brought you here to make: connections. A person who is worth nothing must introduce you to a person worth next-to-nothing, and that person to another, and so on and so forth until finally you can step across the threshold, almost one of the family.

From *The Crimson Petal and the White* by Michael Faber, published by Canongate Books, 2002.

ISBN: 9780170415965

2 Record your first impressions below and, on the extract, circle or highlight any words you are unfamiliar with.

_____

_____

_____

3 VOCABULARY

Find the definition for your words that makes sense for this text. Write that definition in the space provided.

Word 1: _____ _____

Word 2: _____ _____

Word 3: _____ _____

4 IMAGERY

Writers use particular words to help us build pictures in our minds. This is called imagery. Often writers use the five senses to make the setting and/or characters believable.

a Look through the text again. Every time you find words or phrases that refer to a sense, copy them into the chart below. We have done some to help you.
Taste does not feature in this extract so don't look for it.

Sense	Words/phrases (quote from text)
Sight	blacking-grey haze of my own spent breath
Sound/hearing	
Touch/feel	uneven ground
Smell	

b Which sense has Faber used the most? _____

c Why is this effective in making you feel like you are in the story?

_____

_____

_____

_____

ISBN: 9780170415965

Identifying the 'point of change'

G *This extract has two points of change, rather than just one. The first is a change in the **tone** and the second helps us to understand the purpose of starting the novel this way.*

1 Read the extract again.

2 You will see that the start of each paragraph is indicated by an indent. Identify the paragraph in which we see the first point of change. _____

3 What is the effect of the phrase 'And yet you did not choose me blindly'?

_____

_____

_____

4 There is another change later on. Identify the paragraph in which this second change occurs in. Write down the sentence.

_____

_____

5 Describe how this change alters your perception of the book.

_____

_____

G **6** Identify one **phrase** that contributes to our understanding of the author's purpose.

_____

_____

_____

_____

> **G** **Phrase:** a sequence of two or more words working together as a single image or idea.

ISBN: 9780170415965

Identifying how the text is communicated

Remember, the choice of words and phrases helps communicate the author's attitude to what they are writing about.

features = techniques

1   The following **language features** can be found in the text. Find and label on the text (on page 24) an example of each of the techniques in the box below.

imperative	contrast	adjective	parallel structure
repetition	metaphor	personal pronoun	personification
simile	compound words	rhetorical question	alliteration

2   Choose three of the techniques you have labelled and fill in the following chart. We have done an example for you.

Technique	Example	Effect
personal pronoun	'Watch your step.'	Direct address from the book to the reader. The effect is to make us feel it is written directly to us and therefore we pay more attention.

3   This extract is written as direct address. This affects the tone. Identify the tone.

_____

_____

4   What is the effect of this tone on the reader?

_____

_____

_____

_____

ISBN: 9780170415965

Putting it all together

Now that you have spent some time 'unpacking' the extract, recognising its language features, and thought about the effects, the meaning and the author's purpose, it's time to put all the parts together and practise writing the types of answers you will need to write in your examination. You can use the notes you have made in the previous pages to help you.

1 Select (✓) ONE language feature the writer uses to describe the setting.

G

- ☐ adjective
- ☐ imperative
- ☐ simile

- ☐ metaphor
- ☐ repetition
- ☐ personal pronoun

- ☐ alliteration
- ☐ rhetorical question
- ☐ personification

2 Give an example of this language feature.

_____

_____

_____

3 Explain how this and/or other language feature(s) help the narrator share **his feelings** towards the **London** he is showing you. You might consider:

- how the description of the physical environment reflects the narrator's feelings
- how a particular mood is created or sustained
- why these details have been selected.

Here are some **possible** sentence starters to help you:

The narrator is describing London as … because …

We see this when the author uses the technique of … when he writes [insert quote] '…'

The effect of this is to emphasise/highlight …

The reason for this is …

Another way this is shown is through the technique of …, which we see in the line [insert different quote] '…'

From this we learn …

It makes us think about … in our own lives because …

Finally, the author wanted us to remember/act/learn that … because … just like in the story when …

_____

_____

_____

_____

_____

_____

_____

_____

_____

_____

NARRATIVE PROSE 4

This is the final text in this section with some activities. Remember to pay particular attention to the language used, the title and the point of change.

Reading the text

1 Read the extract through once, slowly (out loud if you can). Don't do anything else; just read.

Red Pen

Words bear down upon him. They weigh him down till he is broken and hollow, only a shadow of what he once was, what he could have been.

He stares at blank pages beneath him, frowns, plays with his pen drawing lines on his page. Inspiration is not with him today. It does not seem to be with him any day.

There's this silence hanging around the classroom. Like fog — it fills the air and my ears try to breathe it in. Every now and then a page rustles, someone coughs, a light is seen through the dull grey.

It settles down again. I might as well be back home, where the quiet is nicer, well-mannered. It welcomes me in and is only interrupted every now and then by the breeze blowing through the curtains — dropping in, ruffling my hair, leaving again.

I can forget about the world there. Alone, but not lonely, not surrounded by strangers and rustling book pages and coughs.

That well-mannered silence does not exist here. Not even in the library. Not even in the despair-filled English classroom from which I write.

A pen drops, rolling beneath the desk between me and him.

The silence does not exist here, and it sometimes feels like I don't either.

He leans back in his chair, staring at the fallen pen. It's red, the only colour he could bring today. All his other pens have been lost or never returned, and he doesn't feel like buying new ones. His eyes don't really seem to be able to register where it's fallen. He looks the way I feel: exhausted.

I'd like to pretend I know what's going on, like I could help, but there's a distance that's farther than just the space between our chairs, farther than the desk that separates us. It spreads on and on like a vast desert, so that no one can reach him.

The only thing I feel I can do is pick up the pen for him, and set it lightly back down on the empty page of his notebook.

He blinks at it. His eyes flicker up at me and then back down to the pen. I shrug slightly, try to give him a soft — slightly forced — smile, but he's not looking.

Maybe he'll stare at that red pen blankly for the rest of the class. Maybe he'll pick it up and scribble a messy 'hello' onto the paper before pushing his notebook over to me for a reply. I never know what he's going to do.

Maybe, once we escape this awful silence, he'll see the light that I often see when the wind blows through the curtains.

His head might stop being an empty space filled with the quiet coughs and blank pages staring back up at him, mocking him with blue lines blurring together. Maybe all he needs is a bright blue sky or a few days of rain.

I can only hope.

I watch him silently, as he carefully picks up the pen, sets it to the paper, and slowly begins to write.

'Red Pen' by Audrey Philips, Year 12, 2015.

2 Record your first impressions below.

_____

_____

_____

3 **THE TITLE**

Remember that the title of a text tells us a lot about the subject matter and/or the author's purpose.

In the spaces below, write down what ideas or feelings the word suggests to you. (These 'suggestions' are called **connotations**.)

Red _____

_____

Pen _____

_____

4 Reread the text and answer the questions below.

a In no more than three sentences, finish this prompt:

This story is about _____

_____

_____.

b Write down three assumptions you can make about the boy the narrator is describing.

i _____

_____

ii _____

_____

iii _____

_____

c Write down three assumptions you can make about the narrator.

i _____

_____

ii _____

_____

iii _____

_____

d In one sentence, describe the relationship between the narrator and the boy.

_____

_____

_____

Identifying how the text is communicated

1   The following **language features** can be found in the text. Find and label on the text (on page 30) an example of at least five of the techniques in the box. You may find more than one example of some.

> features = techniques

G

metaphor	simile	personification
alliteration	repetition	adjective
parallel construction	onomatopoeia	personal pronoun

2   Choose three of the language features you have labelled and fill in the following chart. We have done an example for you.

Technique	Example	Effect
personification	'blank pages ... mocking him'	Makes the pages come alive and seem that they too are judging the boy for not being able to write on them.

3   This short story is written in the present tense. For example, 'A pen drops, rolling beneath the desk between me and him.' Explain the effect on the reader of using present tense in this story.

_____

_____

_____

_____

_____

_____

Putting it all together

You can use the notes you have made in the previous pages to help you.

1 Select (✓) ONE language feature the author uses to describe the setting of the classroom.

☐ adjective   ☐ metaphor   ☐ alliteration

☐ listing   ☐ repetition   ☐ personification

☐ simile   ☐ onomatopoeia   ☐ compound word

2 Give an example of this language feature.

_____

_____

_____

3 Explain how this and/or other language feature(s) help you to **understand** the narrator's **feelings towards how the boy is coping with the classroom writing activity**. If you get stuck, look back on some of the sentence starters on pages 23 and 28.

Support your answer with reference to the text including language features. You might consider:

- the contrast between how she finds writing in class and writing at home
- the contrast between the narrator and the boy
- how the mood is created and sustained through her description of the boy.

_____

_____

_____

_____

_____

_____

_____

_____

_____

_____

_____

_____

_____

_____

_____

ISBN: 9780170415965

NARRATIVE PROSE 5

Now that you have completed the first four fiction texts, you are ready to attempt a piece as if you were under exam conditions.

Using all of the skills you have been practising throughout this chapter, give this your best shot.

Put your timer on for 20 minutes. Read the piece, use your strategies and answer the questions. Good luck!

Third Degree
[Ten-year-old Ruth is in the intensive care ward of the hospital because she has sustained third degree burns.]

I know this room well. I have decorated the walls in my mind and I can see shapes in the peeling paint: horses and dogs and clouds and a funny man. I have watched unicorns dancing with snakes and seen them change. Because I have to lie still, 'Lie still!' all the time while the nurses pull strips of skin from my body. They use plastic tweezers with nasty ridges of teeth. One nurse has shown this to me and told me why they have to pick, and jab, and pull and tug at the bits of flesh that lie dead on my body.

My oldest brother comes to visit me. I feel shy because I have no clothes on and no sheet to hide my nakedness. He smiles and chats about my cat sleeping on my pillow; about the hut in the haybarn; about telling them at school where I am. He chats but he does not look at me though I look at him. Look at him standing near the window, looking out; standing near the unicorn and the man in the funny hat. I wonder if I should point it out to him but I do not want to seem childish so I say nothing. Like the others, he wears a mask.

My mother comes to visit me. She tells me about my cat sleeping on my pillow, about the new farmhand, about the cake she'd made for me and would have given me but the nurses took it from her. She holds my hand and asks me how I am. 'Fine,' I say. 'I am fine.' Then a nurse comes to pluck at my body again and Mum has to leave.

The nurse starts with my face, on my forehead. She lays a small cloth on my shoulder and, as she pulls off the skin, wipes it on the cloth. She smells of soap and has tight hair. Out of the corner of my eye, I watch the mask suck in and out with her breathing. In front of me, the unicorn's horn has pulled free from the wall and hangs in strips, just like my skin. I want to tell the nurse to take her tweezers and do to the wall what she is doing to me but I am afraid of her. So, I say nothing. Jab, jab, jab, wipe; jab, jab, jab, wipe. She tugs at me roughly and I wonder if she is unhappy, with her tight hair and her cruel fingers. Pinch, pull, tug, wipe. I stare at the clock and watch the hands jump in time to the nurse's work. It jumps for me because I cannot jump.

'Lie still,' I am told though I have not moved. I need to go to the toilet but I have to use a bedpan as I am forbidden to go past the two-doors. Soon, I am busting and I have to tell her. I turn my head to speak just as she reaches up for another piece of skin. The instrument stabs me in the cheek and the pain shoots through me and out the other side. I am crying now, but the nurse is muttering.

'I told you to lie still, you silly girl,' she growls.

'I need to go to the toilet,' I sob.

The nurse snorts, throws the tweezers into a bowl and pushes away from the bed. She does not help me and I go over to the corner of the room and wee into the bedpan, feeling shy, feeling shamed. My cheek tickles and I dab it with the toilet paper. It comes back with blood on it. I look over at the nurse but she is staring out the window, tapping her fingers on the side cabinet. I cover the pan as I have been shown and climb back on the bed. I am still without clothes and I wish I could just have a sheet to cover my lower half. The treatment continues and I close my eyes.

From *Third Degree* by Tania Roxborogh, published by Longacre Press, 2005.

ISBN: 9780170415965

1 Select (✓) ONE language feature the author uses to describe the setting of the hospital room.

☐ adjective ☐ metaphor ☐ alliteration
☐ listing ☐ repetition ☐ personification
☐ simile ☐ parallel structure ☐ incomplete sentence

2 Give an example of this language feature.

_____

_____

_____

3 Explain how this and/or other language feature(s) help you to **understand** the narrator's **feelings about being in hospital**. You might consider:

- what the narrator sees
- how she describes her environment
- what the writer wanted the reader to understand about Ruth's situation.

_____

_____

_____

_____

_____

_____

_____

_____

_____

_____

_____

_____

_____

_____

_____

_____

_____

_____

_____

_____

_____

NARRATIVE PROSE 6

Using all of the skills you have been practising throughout this chapter, give this your best shot.

Put your timer on for 20 minutes. Read the piece, use your strategies and answer the questions. Good luck!

Beach Patrol

The first proper day of our school holiday, I'd dragged Robbie along with me for 'beach patrol' — one of the six tasks in my Sea Cadets service book to complete for the summer. Not the saving-foolish-swimmers kind of patrol but the one which still involved idiots doing dumb things. Today's dumbness was brought to Tolaga Bay from a couple of out-of-towners.

Robbie and I were able to track their movements through the sand dunes to the beach by the discarded RTD bottles, crisp packets and someone's underpants. By the time we found them, our sack was half filled with their droppings.

They were sitting on the beach, their surfboards rammed into the sand like military sentinels. 'Hey,' I called out to them. 'You guys left something back there.' I gave the *hey we're all mates* grin and continued to walk toward them. 'My brother and I have brought it back for you.'

They stood, looking tall, muscly and mean. 'Get lost, kid,' the one with the dreadlocks snarled.

Robbie hovered just behind me and I could hear his quick breathing but we were committed now.

'Nah,' I said. 'Didn't your mothers teach you it's rude to visit someone's place and leave your mess?'

The shaved-headed one took a step toward me. 'Scram before we feed you to the sharks.'

He puffed out his chest; arms and shoulders back like a gorilla then gave me a hard shove so that I stepped back but lost my footing, falling hard onto the sand, flat on my back and staring up at his ugly mug.

'Oh no!' Robbie rushed forward blocking their view of me. 'Charlie,' he said, his voice high and worried but he was grinning as he gave my left leg a hard tug. Then he jumped up. 'Look what you've done,' he cried, face serious, eyes wide, pointing to me.

I groaned loudly and was pleased to see the shocked faces of the older boys.

Baldy looked like he was going to barf.

'Look at his leg, man!' Dreadlocks said, pointing to my left foot, which was now protruding about six inches more from my jeans than my right foot.

'I'm calling the cops,' Robbie shouted and pulled out his phone. 'You're in so much trouble now.'

'Let's get out of here,' Baldy said, pulling his surfboard out of the sand.

I moaned dramatically but, as expected, they continued to pick up their gear. 'You can run but you can't hide,' I said, exaggerating my breathing. 'The police will be able to track you by finger-printing your rubbish.'

That thought seemed to register in their dumb-ass heads and they stopped for a moment, looked at each other, down at me and then at Robbie.

Dreadlocks was obviously the more intelligent one. 'Get the bag,' he barked at Baldy. 'And don't leave any of your stuff here.'

Baldy snatched the seed sack Robbie held out to him and, as an afterthought, grabbed the plastic bag out of my hand and rammed it into the sack.

While I continued to hold my thigh and give the leg a bit of a sickening jiggle, the two older boys scrabbled around, before high-tailing it off the beach, through the dunes and out of sight.

'They've gone,' Robbie said a moment later, pocketing his phone.

'Good one,' I said, rolling up the pants of my jeans. 'Take the foot would you?'

Robbie crouched down and twisted the left foot of my prosthetic leg to the right while I pulled. There was a satisfying click sound and my legs were now the same length.

'Give us a hand,' I said.

Robbie grabbed my arms. 'Don't you mean, 'leg'?' Old joke, still made him laugh.

'Beach Patrol' from *Charlie Tangaroa and the Creature from the Sea* by T.K. Roxborogh.

ISBN: 9780170415965

1 Select (✓) ONE language feature the author uses to describe the meeting between the boys and the surfers.

- ☐ adjective
- ☐ listing
- ☐ simile
- ☐ metaphor
- ☐ repetition
- ☐ onomatopoeia
- ☐ alliteration
- ☐ colloquial language
- ☐ compound word

2 Give an example from the text.

_____

_____

_____

3 Explain how this and/or other language feature(s) help you **understand the highs and lows of the action in the text**. You might consider:

- the language used to describe the surfers
- the narrator's feelings towards the surfers
- how the narrator reacts to what happens.

_____

_____

_____

_____

_____

_____

_____

_____

_____

_____

_____

_____

_____

_____

_____

_____

_____

_____

Section **Two:** POETRY

Eighteenth-century poet Alexander Pope once explained the difference between poetry and other forms of writing. He said: *Prose: the **best** words. Poetry: the **best** words in the **best order***.

Poems can be written to sound beautiful, to tell a story or to share a message. They are designed to recreate the emotional response and/or experience of the poet for the reader. In analysing poetry, *how* the ideas are communicated is just as important as what the ideas are. The poet specifically pays attention to:

- structure and rhythm
- form
- tone
- word choice
- and all of those things that create the effect the poet is trying to achieve.

Approach the study of poetry with an understanding that poems are like icebergs — they can be enjoyed for their beauty if you see them from just the surface, but a total appreciation of their awesomeness is seen only when you dive down and look beneath.

POETRY 1

Pre-reading activities

As with the narrative prose/fiction chapter, before you read the poem, let's prepare by looking at some words that might be new to you. Next, we will consider any ideas you may already have about some others. Finally, we will look at ways to 'predict' the subject and purpose of a poem.

1 VOCABULARY WORK

Look up the following words in a dictionary and write the most common meaning beside it.

a emblem _____

_____

b reminiscent _____

_____

c papyrus _____

_____

d blotch _____

_____

e lavender _____

_____

ISBN: 9780170415965

2 THE TITLE

The title of a poem is often a **metaphor** and is a helpful clue to understand the poet's overall purpose for writing the poem. It is worth spending a bit of time working out what the title might mean. The following is the title of your first poem: *My Sister's Top*.

a In the spaces below, write down the **literal** (dictionary) definition of the word and then, beside it, what ideas or feelings the word suggests to you. (These 'suggestions' are called **connotations**.)

My   belonging to the speaker   *feeling possessive — it belongs to me, no one else*

Sister's _____

_____

Top _____

_____

_____

b Finish the sentence below. To help you with your answer, use the vocabulary and thinking from **1** and **2** above.

I think the poem will be about _____

_____

because _____

_____

_____

> **The magic 'because'**
> The word 'because' is a magic word as it forces us to explain and justify our statement.

3 PREDICTING VOCABULARY

Looking at **1** and **2** and your answers above, predict two *different* words you think might appear in this poem. For each word, give a reason why you think this might be. We have done an example for you.

argument _____ because _*I think the poet spoiled her sister's good top and the sister is angry*_

a _____ because _____

_____

_____

_____

b _____ because _____

_____

_____

_____

Reading the poem

1 Read the poem through once, slowly (out loud if you can). Don't do anything else; just read.

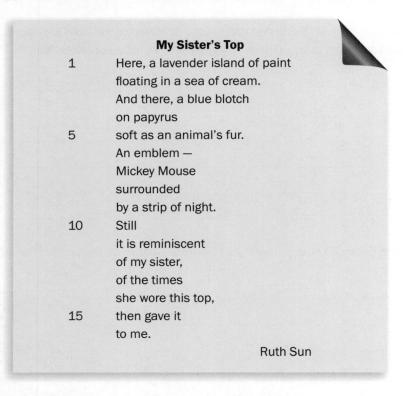

My Sister's Top

1   Here, a lavender island of paint
     floating in a sea of cream.
     And there, a blue blotch
     on papyrus
5   soft as an animal's fur.
     An emblem —
     Mickey Mouse
     surrounded
     by a strip of night.
10   Still
     it is reminiscent
     of my sister,
     of the times
     she wore this top,
15   then gave it
     to me.

                    Ruth Sun

2 Use the space below to record your first impressions of the poem. You can write in bullet points, draw some images or write in full sentences.

3 Read the poem again. Look at your prediction on the previous page, then complete the following statements:

I was correct when I predicted _____.

I was incorrect when I predicted _____ I think this is

because _____

_____.

One thing that surprised me about the poem was _____

_____

_____.

> Don't forget to include a magic 'because' in your answer.

ISBN: 9780170415965

Using the 'Three Level Reading Guide'

This guide will help you to gain a deeper understanding of the poem, starting with the basics and going towards a deeper analysis of the poem.

Level One: **Literal** meanings or 'on the surface' statements. The information can easily be found in the text.

Level Two: **Interpretation** of the Level One statements, or 'between the lines'. You say what you think the writer means using your understanding of the information provided.

Level Three: **Application** of the ideas by 'going beyond the lines'. You make judgements based on the information in the text and your own interpretations.

1   Read each statement below and circle whether it is TRUE or FALSE. (Thinking about these statements will help you gain a deeper understanding of the poem.)

Level One: **Literal** meanings or 'on the surface' statements.

a	The top has paint stains.	TRUE/FALSE
b	It was the brother's top.	TRUE/FALSE
c	The top is made from animal fur.	TRUE/FALSE
d	The top is orange.	TRUE/FALSE
e	The sister wore the top.	TRUE/FALSE

Level Two: **Interpretation** of the Level One statements or 'between the lines'.

a	This is a child's top.	TRUE/FALSE
b	This top was a gift to the poet.	TRUE/FALSE
c	Mickey Mouse is floating on the sea.	TRUE/FALSE
d	This top is too small for the poet.	TRUE/FALSE
e	The top reminds the poet of her sister.	TRUE/FALSE

Level Three: **Application** of the ideas by 'going beyond the lines'.

a	The family struggles for money.	TRUE/FALSE
b	The poet is resentful of her sister.	TRUE/FALSE
c	The sister no longer lives at home.	TRUE/FALSE
d	The top was bought at Disneyland.	TRUE/FALSE
e	The poet has a vivid imagination.	TRUE/FALSE

2   Choose one of the Level Three statements (going beyond the lines) that you believe is true and explain why you think it is true. Use evidence from the poem to support your answer.

Letter: _____

This is true because _____

_____

_____.

ISBN: 9780170415965

Identifying the 'point of change'

Remember how we said that all narrative prose/fiction has a point of change in it (see, for example, pages 12 and 21)? Well, poetry is another form of fiction. Identifying the point of change in an unfamiliar text will provide you with a clear idea to discuss and help you to write a more insightful answer in the examination.

1 Read the poem through again. Line numbers are indicated down the left-hand side. Identify in which line or lines

the point of change occurs: _____

Now, you can see that the poem is divided into two halves.

2 What is the main idea in the first half?

_____

_____

3 What is the main idea in the second half?

_____

_____

4 What do you think caused the change?

_____

_____

_____

Linking the title with the end of the poem

A wee trick also to help with understanding the overall purpose of a poem is to read only the title and last line(s) together and consider this as the idea or event that has motivated the poet to write their poem. It can also help you to identify the tone or attitude of the poet towards the subject of their poem.

1 Write down the title and the last two lines of the poem.

_____

_____

_____

2 What might the information above tell you about the poet's attitude to the sister/the sister's top?

_____

_____

_____

_____

_____

_____

ISBN: 9780170415965

Identifying how the poem is communicated

*The choice of words and phrases helps communicate the poet's attitude to what they are writing about. Identifying the **tone** of a passage will help you understand the author's purpose in writing the text. Ideas are communicated through a variety of **language features or language techniques**. These terms are used interchangeably in this book.*

Visual		Sound
simile	metaphor	rhyme
personification	adjective	rhythm
adverb	repetition	alliteration
hyperbole	listing	onomatopoeia

Fill in the following grid about the ideas in the poem and what **techniques** help communicate these ideas — we have started it off for you.

What idea?	Technique	Evidence	Explain the effect and/or purpose
The top is old and stained	noun	'blotch'	'blotch' means uneven, a mistake; the word helps to describe what the top looks like.
The top reminds the poet of her sister			
	alliteration		

Putting it all together

Now that you have spent some time 'unpacking' the poem, recognising its language features, and thought about the effects, the meaning and the poet's purpose, it's time to put all the parts together again and practise writing the types of answers you will need to write in your examination. You can use the notes you have made in the previous pages to help you.

1 Select (✓) ONE language feature the author uses to describe the top.

☐ adjective ☐ simile ☐ rhyme
☐ personal pronoun ☐ metaphor ☐ alliteration

2 Give an example from the text.

_____

_____

3 Write a paragraph explaining how this and/or other language feature(s) help you **understand** the poet's **attitude towards her sister's gift**. Consider:
- the language used to describe the top
- the poet's feelings towards her sister
- the main purpose of the poem.

We have included starter sentences for your paragraph. Complete each sentence thoroughly and you will have a great paragraph answer.

The poet is saying that even though the top is old and stained, she feels _____

towards her sister's gift.

We see this attitude when the poet uses the technique of _____

when he writes [insert quote] '_____

_____ ,

The effect of this is to emphasise/highlight _____

_____ .

The reason for this is _____

_____

_____ .

Another way this attitude is shown is through the use of _____ ,

which we see in the text where it says [insert different quote] '_____

_____ ,

_____ .

From this we learn _____

_____

_____ .

It makes us think about _____

_____

ISBN: 9780170415965

because _____

_____

_____.

Finally, the poet wanted us to remember/act/learn that _____

_____

_____

_____

because _____

_____

_____

_____

just like in the poem when _____

_____

_____.

ISBN: 9780170415965

POETRY 2

Pre-reading activities

1 VOCABULARY WORK

Match up the following definitions and terms.

Term	Definition
agitated	a group of people who think of new ideas on a particular subject
think tank	a backward flow or movement produced especially by a propelling force
wharf post	a mass of large seaweeds
back wash	to find the way to get to a place when you are travelling
navigate	moved or stirred up
kelp	part of a structure to which boats are tied, immovable and permanent

2 THE TITLE

Poets are deliberate in their choice of words; one reason is because poems are generally short, and every word needs to be the most appropriate word. It is worth considering why a poet might choose one word over another.

The title of this next poem is **Invigilator**.

Here is the definition *and* a synonym for this word:

invigilator — a person in a position of trust who is present to uphold the conduct of students sitting an exam in order to check that all conditions are equal throughout the country and that nobody cheats.

supervisor — someone who watches over a person or an activity to make certain that everything is done safely and correctly.

a   Why do you think the poet might have chosen the word 'invigilator' over the word 'supervisor' for the title?

_____

_____

b   What thing or activity could the word 'invigilator' be compared to (what could be a metaphor)?

_____

3 PREDICTING VOCABULARY

This is such a specific word for the title. What do you think this poem might be about?

_____

_____

_____

_____

Don't forget to include a magic 'because' in your answer.

ISBN: 9780170415965

Reading the poem

1 Read the poem through once, slowly (out loud if you can). Don't do anything else; just read.

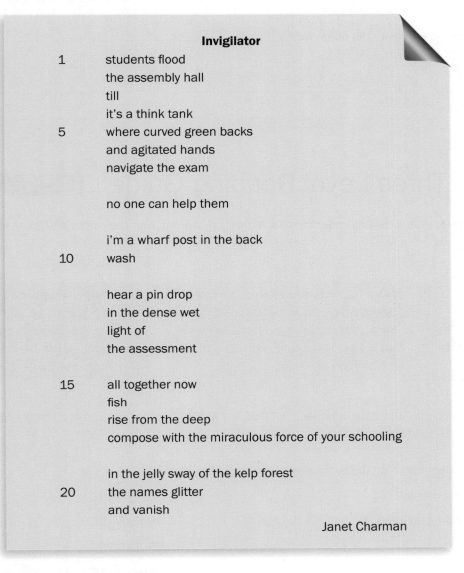

Invigilator

1	students flood
	the assembly hall
	till
	it's a think tank
5	where curved green backs
	and agitated hands
	navigate the exam
	no one can help them
	i'm a wharf post in the back
10	wash
	hear a pin drop
	in the dense wet
	light of
	the assessment
15	all together now
	fish
	rise from the deep
	compose with the miraculous force of your schooling
	in the jelly sway of the kelp forest
20	the names glitter
	and vanish

Janet Charman

2 Use the space below to record your first impressions of the poem.

ISBN: 9780170415965

3 Read the poem again. Look at your prediction on the previous page, then complete the following statements:

I was correct when I predicted _____.

I was incorrect when I predicted _____ I think this

is because _____.

One thing that surprised me about the poem was _____

_____

_____

_____

Using the 'Three Level Reading Guide'

This guide with help you to gain a deeper understanding of the text, starting with the basics and going towards a deeper analysis of the text.

Level One: **Literal** meanings or 'on the surface' statements. The information can easily be found in the text.	Level Two: **Interpretation** of the Level One statements, or 'between the lines'. You say what you think the writer means using your understanding of the information provided.	Level Three: **Application** of the ideas by 'going beyond the lines'. You make judgements based on the information in the text and your own interpretations.

1 Read each statement below and circle whether it is **TRUE** or **FALSE**. (Thinking about these statements will help you gain a deeper understanding of the text.)

Level One: **Literal** meanings or 'on the surface' statements.

a The narrator is at an exam.   TRUE/FALSE

b The narrator is sitting an exam.   TRUE/FALSE

c It is quiet.   TRUE/FALSE

d The narrator is a wharf post.   TRUE/FALSE

Level Two: **Interpretation** of the Level One statements or 'between the lines'.

a The students are prepared for the exam.   TRUE/FALSE

b The school uniform has green jumpers.   TRUE/FALSE

c The students are actually fish.   TRUE/FALSE

d The narrator wants to help the students pass the exam. TRUE/FALSE

Level Three: **Application** of the ideas by 'going beyond the lines'.

a The narrator doesn't agree with exams.   TRUE/FALSE

b The narrator believes exams let you be an individual. TRUE/FALSE

c The narrator feels helpless against the schooling system. TRUE/FALSE

d The narrator thinks students are capable of coping with exams. TRUE/FALSE

2 Choose one of the Level Three statements (going beyond the lines) that you believe is true and explain why you think it is true. Use evidence from the text to support your answer:

Letter: _____

This is true because _____

_____

_____

_____

_____ .

Identifying the 'point of change'

Remember that the 'point of change' is key to unlocking the author's purpose.

1 Identify the point of change in the poem according to the line number(s). _____

G

2 What is the **tone (attitude)** in the first part of the poem?

_____

_____

3 What is the **tone (attitude)** after the point of change?

_____

_____

4 What is the reason for the change? Give specific examples from the poem to support your point.

_____

_____

_____

Identifying how the poem is communicated

The choice of words and phrases helps communicate the poet's attitude to what they are writing about. Identifying the **tone** *of a passage will help you understand the author's purpose in writing the text. Ideas are communicated through a variety of* **language features or language techniques**. *These terms are used interchangeably in this book.*

1 Complete the following grid of **language features**:

Term	Example	Effect
metaphor	students flood the assembly hall	lots of students/too many/uncontrolled/a bit frightening
alliteration		
metaphor		old, weather-beaten, been around for a long time, immovable despite all the movement of the tides coming and going/ students sitting exams every year
assonance	**ag**itated h**an**ds	
pun		
cliché		we all know the meaning of this overused phrase and that it means so quiet
personification/ metaphor		like stars/stand out/in contrast to the idea of them all being like each other (school of fish moving in the same way)

ISBN: 9780170415965

2 VISUALISATION EXERCISE

Use the frames below to sketch the four events of the poem.

a Read the poem again, paying particular attention to the **water references**.

b In each of the above boxes, add in the water reference that relates to your drawing. Put it in quote marks.

c The repeated images comparing the students and their exam to the sea is called an **extended metaphor**. Why might a poet use an extended metaphor? What could it add to a poem for the reader?

> **Extended metaphor:** This term refers to a comparison between two unlike things that continues throughout a series of sentences in a paragraph or lines in a poem.

_____

_____

_____

_____

d The poet has chosen *not* to use any capital letters, commas or full stops in her poem. Thinking about the *purpose* of these punctuation marks, what is the effect of not having these in the poem?

_____

_____

_____

_____

e Now thinking about the main message of the poem, how does this technique *add* to our understanding of the poem?

_____

_____

_____

_____

Putting it all together

Now that you have spent some time 'unpacking' the poem, recognising its language features, and thought about the effects, the meaning and the poet's purpose, it's time to put all the parts together and practise writing the types of answers you will need to write in your examination. You can use the notes you have made in the previous pages to help you.

1 Select (✓) ONE language feature the author uses to describe the setting.

☐ adjective   ☐ assonance   ☐ use of punctuation
☐ metaphor   ☐ pun   ☐ cliché
☐ alliteration   ☐ personal pronoun

2 Give an example from the text.

_____

_____

3 Explain how this and/or other language feature(s) help you to **understand** the poet's **experience of the exam** throughout the text. Consider:
- the poet's feelings about the exam
- what the extended metaphor does for the topic
- the poet's overall attitude towards learning.

We have included starter sentences for your paragraph. Complete each sentence thoroughly and you will have a great paragraph answer:

The poet is saying that her experience of the exam is _____

_____

_____

We see this attitude when the poet uses the technique of_____

when she writes [insert quote] '_____ ' .

The effect of this is to emphasise/highlight _____

_____

The reason for this is _____

_____

_____

Another way this experience is shown is through the technique of _____ ,

which we see in the line [insert different quote] '_____

_____ ' .

From this we learn _____

_____

ISBN: 9780170415965

It makes us think about _____

_____

in our own lives _____

_____

_____.

Finally, the poet wanted us to remember/act/learn that _____

_____

because _____

_____

_____

just like in the poem when _____

_____

_____.

POETRY 3

Now that you have worked through two poetry texts, we will be starting to remove some of the activities. This doesn't mean that they are no longer important, but, rather, we are hoping that you are starting to work through them naturally yourself as you read the text. Remember to pay attention to the language used, the title and your first impressions.

Reading the poem

1   Read the poem through once, slowly (out loud if you can). Don't do anything else; just read.

> **Tooth**
>
> 1   Today, you're twelve teeth old,
>   and we fossick for shells,
>   star-fish, pipi and paua
>
>   until the tide goes out
> 5   when we wave goodbye
>   to yachts moored in the marina.
>
>   At home, you float
>   across polished floors
>   until you keel over.
>
> 10   Your jaw leaves an alveolus
>   in the matai deep enough
>   for a tear-drop's caress.
>
>   As I stroke you,
>   your eyes collect water;
> 15   your gums are an ocean of blood.
>
>   But only when you're sleeping,
>   do I discover a tooth
>   anchored to blue woollen blanket.
>
>   Suddenly, you're eleven teeth old
> 20   and have grown, like Lazarus,
>   younger beneath moonlight.
>
>   White and hull-shaped,
>   tooth's a boat,
>   isolated by low tide.
>
> 25   In the morning,
>   I'll show you how it can rest
>   safely upon its starboard.
>
>   Siobhan Harvey

About this poem
Siobhan Harvey is a New Zealand poet. She wrote this poem after her eldest child lost a tooth.

ISBN: 9780170415965   PHOTOCOPYING OF THIS PAGE IS RESTRICTED UNDER LAW.

2 Record your first impressions below.

_____

_____

_____

_____

3 VOCABULARY WORK

a Circle or highlight any words in the poem you are unfamiliar with.

b Use a dictionary or your device to find the definition for your words (from task **a**) that makes sense for this poem. Write that definition in the space provided.

Word 1: _____ _____

_____

Word 2: _____ _____

_____

Word 3: _____ _____

_____

4 MAKING CONNECTIONS

Making connections is when you make a link or association between what you read and your own prior knowledge. There are three types: Text to Text; Text to Self; Text to World.

Stanza 7:

Suddenly, you're eleven teeth old
*and have grown, **like Lazarus**,*
younger beneath moonlight.

> **Stanza:** a grouping of lines in a poem similar to verses in a song. **G**

> Here, Harvey is referencing a *Dr Who* episode where a character goes into a machine and comes out younger. The original Lazarus is from a story in the Bible where Jesus raises him from the dead.

Now that you know the **Text to World** connection that Harvey has made, what is your interpretation of stanza 7?

_____

_____

_____

_____

_____

_____

Identifying the 'point of change'

This poem is unusual in that it has two points of change, rather than just one. The first is a change in the **atmosphere** *and the second is a change in the* **poet's understanding** *of things.*

1 Identify the line where the first point of change occurs. _____

2 Identify the line where the second point of change occurs. _____

3 Describe the atmosphere in the first three **stanzas** of the poem.

_____

_____

4 Identify two words that contribute to this atmosphere. _____ _____

5 Describe the atmosphere in stanzas 4–6 of the poem.

_____

_____

6 Identify one **phrase** that contributes to this atmosphere.

_____

7 Describe the atmosphere in the last three stanzas of the poem.

_____

_____

Identifying how the poem is communicated

1 The following **language features** can be found in the poem. Find and label on the poem (on page 54) an example of each of the techniques in the box below.

features = techniques

alliteration	metaphor	adjective
personal pronoun	listing	simile
direct address	extended metaphor	personification

ISBN: 9780170415965

2 Choose **three** of the **features/techniques** you have labelled on the poem and fill in the following chart. We have done one for you.

Feature	Example	Effect
personal pronoun	you're	Direct address to the subject of the poem/feels personal.

3 This poem also includes an **extended metaphor**: consistent reference to the sea and boating. With a different coloured pen, go back to the poem and underline every reference to the sea and boating.

4 What are these references to sea and boating being compared to?

_____

5 What is the effect of this extended metaphor?

It helps the reader understand _____

because _____ so that we

might think about _____.

Putting it all together

Now that you have spent some time 'unpacking' the poem, recognising its language features, and thought about the effects, the meaning and the poet's purpose, it's time to put all the parts together and practise writing the types of answers you will need to write in your examination. You can use the notes you have made in the previous pages to help you.

1 Select (✓) ONE language feature the author uses to describe the setting.

☐ alliteration   ☐ metaphor   ☐ adjective
☐ personal pronoun   ☐ listing   ☐ simile
☐ direct address   ☐ extended metaphor ☐ personification

2 Give an example from the text.

_____

_____

ISBN: 9780170415965

3 Explain how this and/or other language feature(s) help you to **understand** the poet's **feelings on the loss of her child's tooth**. You might consider:

- how the description of the physical environment reflects the poet's feelings
- how a particular mood is created or sustained
- what the poet has learned through this experience.

Here are some **possible** sentence starters to help you.

The poet is saying that her feelings on the loss of her child's tooth are …

We see these feelings when the poet uses the technique of … when she writes [insert quote] '…'

The effect of this is to emphasise/highlight …

The reason for this is …

Another way these feelings are shown is through the technique of …, which we see in the line [insert different quote] '…'

From this we learn …

It makes us think about … in our own lives …

Finally, the poet wanted us to remember/act/learn that … because … just like in the poem when …

_____

_____

_____

_____

_____

_____

_____

_____

_____

_____

_____

_____

_____

_____

_____

_____

_____

_____

_____

_____

ISBN: 9780170415965

POETRY 4

This is the final text in this section with some activities. Remember to pay particular attention to the language used, the title and the point of change.

Reading the poem

1   Read the poem through once, slowly (out loud if you can). Don't do anything else; just read.

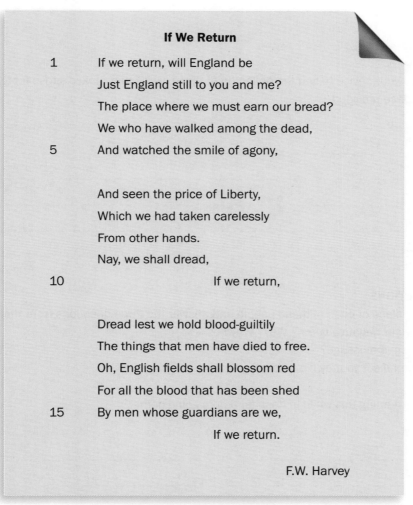

If We Return

1	If we return, will England be
	Just England still to you and me?
	The place where we must earn our bread?
	We who have walked among the dead,
5	And watched the smile of agony,
	And seen the price of Liberty,
	Which we had taken carelessly
	From other hands.
	Nay, we shall dread,
10	If we return,
	Dread lest we hold blood-guiltily
	The things that men have died to free.
	Oh, English fields shall blossom red
	For all the blood that has been shed
15	By men whose guardians are we,
	If we return.

F.W. Harvey

The Penguin Book of First World War Poetry, Penguin Books, 2014.

About this poem

Harvey signed up as a soldier four days after the UK declared war in 1914 and he wrote poems as a release when he moved to France in the spring of 1915. His poetry was published in a trench newspaper and circulated to the soldiers as a morale boost. Captured as a prisoner of war in August 1916, F.W. Harvey spent the remainder of the war in prison camps.

This poem, *If We Return*, was one of Harvey's most famous pieces. It explores the issue of what soldiers would face upon their return to England.

2 Complete the list below. Write six things you know, think you know or can assume about what war veterans must have thought/felt/had happen to them when they came home.

'War veterans coming home'

1 _____

2 _____

3 _____

4 _____

5 _____

6 _____

3 VOCABULARY WORK

Use a dictionary or your device to find the definition of these words that makes sense for this poem. Write that definition in the space provided.

a liberty _____

b blossom _____

c agony _____

d carelessly _____

e guardians _____

f earn _____

4 MAKING CONNECTIONS

Put yourself in the place of each of these people and answer the three questions **from their perspective**.

a Is this a positive or negative poem? Why? Why not?

b What is the poem's message?

c Does this poem reflect your own opinions?

A returning soldier reading this while in hospital before going home:

a _____

_____

_____

b _____

_____

c _____

_____

A teenager living in England during the war:

a _____

_____

_____

b _____

_____

c _____

_____

The poet himself:

a _____

_____

_____

b _____

_____

c _____

_____

Identifying the 'point of change'

This poem is in two parts, where part one asks a question and part two provides the answer.

1 Identify the line where the point of change occurs. _____

2 Describe what the poet is asking in the first part of the poem.

_____

_____

_____

3 Identify the tone of this section of the poem.

Tone: _____

Evidence from the text: _____

_____

4 Describe the tone in the second part of the poem.

_____

_____

_____

G **5** Identify one **phrase** that contributes to this tone.

_____

Identifying how the poem is communicated

1 The following **language features** can be found in the poem. Find and label on the poem (on page 59) an example of each of the techniques in the box below.

> features = techniques

G

alliteration	metaphor	adjective
personal pronoun	repetition	rhyme
rhetorical question	personification	

2 Choose three of the techniques you have labelled and fill in the following chart. We have done one for you.

Language feature	Example	Effect
personal pronoun	'we'	Direct address to the audience makes us feel like we have to consider the poet's question about our own experience of war.

Putting it all together

You can use the notes you have made in the previous pages to help you.

1 Select (✓) ONE language feature the poet uses to describe his attitude towards returning soldiers.

☐ alliteration	☐ metaphor	☐ adjective
☐ personal pronoun	☐ repetition	☐ rhyme
☐ rhetorical question	☐ personification	

2 Give an example from the text.

_____

_____

3 Explain how this and/or other language feature(s) help you to **understand** how the poet communicates **his feelings of returning home after war**. You might consider:

- how the description of the England reflects the poet's feelings
- how a particular mood is created or sustained
- what the poet wants others to understand through this experience of going to war.

_____

_____

_____

_____

_____

_____

_____

_____

_____

_____

_____

_____

_____

_____

_____

_____

_____

_____

_____

_____

POETRY 5

Using all of the skills you have been practising throughout this chapter, give this your best shot.

Put your timer on for 20 minutes. Read the piece, use your strategies and answer the questions. Good luck!

Morning

1   Why do we bother with the rest of the day,
the swale of the afternoon,
the sudden dip into evening,

then night with his notorious perfumes,
5   his many-pointed stars?

this is the best —
throwing off the light covers,
feet on the cold floor,
and buzzing around the house on espresso —

10   maybe a splash of water on the face,
a palmful of vitamins —
but mostly buzzing around the house on espresso,

dictionary and atlas open on the rug,
the typewriter waiting for the key of the head,
15   a cello on the radio,

and, if necessary, the windows —
trees fifty, a hundred years old
out there,
heavy clouds on the way
20   and the lawn steaming like a horse
in the early morning.

Billy Collins

1 Select (✓) ONE language feature the poet uses to describe the morning's activities.

☐ onomatopoeia   ☐ adjective   ☐ personal pronoun

☐ simile   ☐ rhetorical question   ☐ repetition

☐ personification   ☐ parallel structure

2 Give an example from the text.

_____

_____

3 Explain how this and/or other language feature(s) help you to **understand** the poet's **attitude towards morning**. You might consider:

- how the description of the physical environment reflects the poet's feelings
- how a particular mood is created or sustained
- what the poet wants us to realise about early mornings or the start of day.

_____

_____

_____

_____

_____

_____

_____

_____

_____

_____

_____

_____

_____

_____

_____

_____

_____

_____

_____

POETRY 6

Using all of the skills you have been practising throughout this chapter, give this your best shot.

Put your timer on for 20 minutes. Read the piece, use your strategies and answer the questions. Good luck!

A Work of Artifice

1   The bonsai tree
    in the attractive pot
    could have grown eighty feet tall
    on the side of a mountain
5   till split by lightning.
    But a gardener
    carefully pruned it.
    It is nine inches high.
    Every day as he
10 whittles back the branches
    the gardener croons,
    It is your nature
    to be small and cosy,
    domestic and weak;
15 how lucky, little tree,
    to have a pot to grow in.
    With living creatures
    one must begin very early
    to dwarf their growth:
20 the bound feet,
    the crippled brain,
    the hair in curlers,
    the hands you
    love to touch.

Marge Piercy

About this poem

Marge Piercy, a Jewish American writer, born in 1936, is a significant feminist voice. Her work shows commitment to the dream of social change, what she might call 'the repair of the world'. This poem was written at a time when women were expected to stay at home and raise the family, and was in response to a commercial advertising hand lotion for women with the theme 'for the hands you love to touch'.

1 Select (✓) ONE language feature the poet uses to describe the morning's activities.

- [ ] adjective
- [ ] personal pronoun
- [ ] contrast
- [ ] onomatopoeia
- [ ] personification
- [ ] allusion
- [ ] listing
- [ ] parallel structure

2 Give an example from the text.

----

3 Explain how this and/or other language feature(s) help you to **understand** the poet's **attitude towards the gardener**. You might consider:

- what the gardener does with the bonsai
- the reason for the choice and pairing of words
- why the poet has chosen to express her ideas in this way.

Section Three: NON-FICTION

One good thing about analysing a piece of unfamiliar **non-fiction** is that, because the writing is usually more explicit, the topic and purpose is much more obvious to the reader: the author wants to *teach* you something or *persuade* you to agree with them or *motivate* you to action. Oftentimes, it is all of these. Being successful in achieving their intended purpose matters to the writer.

In this chapter, we are going to specifically look at:

- **what** is said in the piece (the subject matter or topic)
- **how** it is said (what language techniques are used and the effect of using these), and
- **why** it is said (the writer's purpose and attitude towards the topic they are writing/speaking about).

NON-FICTION 1

Pre-reading activities

Before you read the text, let's prepare by looking at some words that might be new to you. Next, we will look at ways to 'predict' the subject and purpose of a text.

1 VOCABULARY WORK

Look up the meaning of the following words and write the most common meaning beside it.

a scooter _____

_____

b intricate _____

_____

c fete _____

_____

d incomprehensible _____

_____

e estimated _____

_____

f recruited _____

_____

g invaluable _____

_____

h denied _____

_____

i campaign _____

_____

ISBN: 9780170415965   PHOTOCOPYING OF THIS PAGE IS RESTRICTED UNDER LAW.

After considering these definitions, what do you think might be the subject matter of the text?

I think the piece will be about _____

because _____

_____

_____ .

2   THE TITLE

The title of our first non-fiction text is 'At Ten Years Old'.

a   Write down two memories you have for the time you were ten.

Example: *Watching Justin Bieber with my family.*

_____

_____

b   What ideas do you think this piece might include?

Example: *What life is like as a ten-year-old.*

_____

_____

c   Write your prediction:

I think the piece will be about _____

because _____

_____ .

3   THE BACKGROUND/CONTEXT OF THE EXTRACT

When you read a text, it is important that you take into consideration all the available information: who the author is (male, female, non-binary, transgender, age, nationality, occupation, religion, politics, and so on), when the text was written, where the text is based, and any other details provided, as this can go some way to assisting you in understanding the purpose of the text.

  In the exam, this information is usually provided within the question, and in the small print under the text.

Abridged: (of a book, film, poem) shortened without losing the main sense of it.

'At Ten Years Old' is the text of a speech that was delivered by a sixteen-year-old high school student to her English class. It has been slightly edited and abridged.

a   What things would you expect to be of concern to a sixteen-year-old student?

_____

_____

b   Thinking about the title and your predictions above, what do you think might be the main purpose of the speech?

_____

_____

_____

_____

Reading the text

1 Read the non-fiction piece through once, slowly (out loud if you can). Don't do anything else; just read.

At Ten Years Old

At ten years old my days were filled with trips down to our local beach, riding my scooter around the block with neighbourhood kids, and building intricate tents made of sheets, and pillows. At ten years old Juliet was taken against her will, from her family, from her friends, her education, school, and community. Everything that was dear to her slipped through her fingers in an instant.

At ten years old I remember having my face painted by a senior school pupil down the road at our local fete. At ten years old Juliet remembers painting her face with thick black tiger stripes, ready for battle.

I remember music, dancing around my bedroom to the latest pop tracks. Juliet remembers music too, the echo of the drum beat as she marched one foot in front of the other into battle, with the rest of her troops.

I remember building mud huts, and play-fighting with the boys at school, water fights, water balloons, and laughter. Juliet remembers building mud forts. She remembers real fighting, with men twice her size, grenades, and silences of death.

Juliet is a child who was denied a childhood, forced to spend the days that we all spent playing, fighting for her life. To us, Juliet's childhood is incomprehensible, and it may seem as though this kind of story is uncommon, yet sadly it's quite the opposite. In countries like the Congo and Afghanistan 300,000 child soldiers are estimated to be in combat as we speak, and another 500,000 are recruited ready to face war.

Awareness is invaluable, and from my speech I would like for you to become more aware. For you to understand that not all children are as lucky as we are. That some children are denied a childhood, children like Juliet.

Today I will leave you Juliet's story, a story of war, sadness. I will also leave you with a challenge, make the time to donate to Child Soldiers International and support their campaign to stop the recruitment of all children for war.

Caitlin Addison, Year 12, 2013.

2 FIRST IMPRESSIONS

Read the text through again.

Think: What does the speaker want us to think about/do/join/change, and so on?

Write down one thing we are being encouraged to do as a result of hearing this message.

The speaker wants us to _____

_____

_____

_____ .

ISBN: 9780170415965

Unpacking the text

*In a non-fiction text, whether it be a persuasive piece or a speech, every paragraph contains an idea that relates to the overall purpose. Think about it like a jigsaw, in that each paragraph is a piece that connects to the pieces that come before and after. Looking at the individual pieces is what we call **unpacking the text**.*

1 FIND THE PATTERN

In this task, we want you to look at each paragraph by itself and summarise the idea — the jigsaw piece — in one sentence. Two have been done for you as examples.

Paragraph	Summary
1	Memories of things the narrator did as a child, list of what Juliet lost when she was 10.
2	
3	
4	List of the narrator's happy experience of play fighting, list of Juliet's experiences of war.
5	
6	
7	

It is okay if you write down similar ideas because often the author is repeating their idea in different ways to hammer home their point.

2 SUMMARISE

In no more than *three sentences*, write what this piece is about.

_____

_____

_____

_____

_____

_____

Complete the following sentence:

The writer/speaker wanted to teach us about _____ because

_____

_____

_____

_____

Identifying how the idea is communicated

*Ideas are communicated through a variety of **language features or language techniques** for at least one of the following purposes:*

- *to include the reader*
- *to emphasise a point*
- *to highlight words or ideas*
- *to create a picture in the reader's mind (imagery)*
- *to challenge our thinking*
- *to encourage us to act (call to action).*

> features = techniques

The terms 'features' and 'techniques' are used interchangeably in this book.

1 The following **language features** can be found in the text. Find and label on the text (on page 70) an example of each of the techniques in the box below.

personal pronoun	imperative/command	listing
facts/statistics	contrast	adjective
parallel structure	repetition	anecdote
jargon		

2 Fill in the following grid about the ideas in the text and what language techniques help communicate these ideas. We have started it off for you.

Techniques	Explain the purpose of the technique	Evidence from text of the technique	Explain the effect
statistics	This makes the argument more convincing and believable.	'300,000 child soldiers are estimated to be in combat as we speak, and another 500,000 are recruited'.	As readers, we are appalled at the numbers of children being forced to go to war.
personal pronoun			
listing			
parallel structure		'I remember building mud huts ... Juliet remembers building mud forts'.	
repetition	To draw attention to the word/phrase.		
imperative			

ISBN: 9780170415965

Putting it all together

Now that you have spent some time 'unpacking' the text, recognising its language features, and thought about the effects, the meaning and the author's purpose, it's time to put all the parts together and practise writing the types of answers you will need to write in your examination. You can use the notes you have made in the previous pages to help you.

1 Select (✓) ONE language feature the author uses to set the tone of the piece.

☐ statistics	☐ listing	☐ parallel structure
☐ anecdote	☐ jargon	☐ contrast
☐ repetition	☐ personal pronoun	☐ imperative

2 Give an example from the text.

_____

_____

3 Explain how this and/or other language feature(s) help you **understand** the speaker's **attitude** towards **child soldiers**. You might consider:

- the differences between the lives of the girls
- the words the speaker chooses
- what the overall purpose of the speech is.

We have included starter sentences for your paragraph. Complete each sentence thoroughly and you will have a great paragraph answer.

The speaker's overall purpose in this piece is to _____.

Their attitude towards this topic is _____.

We see this attitude when the speaker uses the technique of _____

when she says [insert quote] '_____'.

The effect of this is to emphasise/highlight _____

_____

_____

The reason for this is _____

_____

_____

because the speaker wants us to _____

Another way this attitude is shown is through the technique of _____,

which we see in the line [insert different quote] '_____

_____'

ISBN: 9780170415965

From this we learn _____.

It makes us think about _____

in our own lives _____.

Finally, the author wanted us to remember/act/learn that _____

_____

_____

because _____

_____

_____

just like in the text when _____

_____

_____

_____.

ISBN: 9780170415965

NON-FICTION 2

Pre-reading activities

1 VOCABULARY WORK

Create a sentence with each of these words in it (their definitions are given in brackets).

a striving (making strenuous efforts towards a goal)

_____

b reconcile (to cause a person to accept something they did not want)

_____

c Tēnā koutou katoa (formal hello to three or more people)

_____

d counsel (advice, especially that given formally)

_____

After considering these definitions, what do you think might be the subject matter of the text?

I think the piece will be about _____

because _____

_____

2 LOOKING AT THE OPENING LINE — THE HOOK

'I wrote a speech and then a week before I was due to deliver it they said, you've got cancer.'

a Why do you think this is a good 'hook'?

_____

_____

b What ideas do you think this speech might include?

_____

_____

c Write your prediction:

I think the speech will be about _____

_____

because _____

_____

ISBN: 9780170415965

3 THE BACKGROUND/CONTEXT OF THE EXTRACT

This is the text of a speech given by Jakob Bailey, the 2015 Senior Monitor (Head Boy) from Christchurch Boys' High School at the occasion of the senior prize giving. The video of the speech has been seen by nearly two million viewers on YouTube. You may have seen it yourself. The text below has been slightly edited and **abridged**.

Thinking about the context and your predictions above, what do you think might be the main message of the speech?

_____

_____

because _____

_____.

Reading the text

1   Read the abridged speech below through once, slowly (out loud if you can). Don't do anything else; just read.

Head Boy's Prizegiving Speech

I wrote a speech and then a week before I was due to deliver it they said, you've got cancer.

They said if you don't get any treatment you'll be dead in three weeks. And they told me that I wouldn't be able to come and deliver this speech here tonight.

But luckily, that speech isn't about what is to come — it's about what an amazing year it has been. And you didn't really expect me to write a whole new one from my hospital bed, did you? It started like this:

Tēnā koutou katoa. Good evening, everyone, I am Jakob Ross Bailey — Senior Monitor* of 2015.

To all the fine young men who have gone before me, and to the fine young men sitting before me, thank you for supporting me as your Senior Monitor this year. Yes, at times I have wondered whether I deserved this job. At times I have doubted I could get it done to the standard I thought it should be done to. But despite my fear, I have never stopped striving to be a leader who did not let you down.

Sadly, it has been both a short and long few years but here we are now, ready to move on, men. We've worked hard to get to this point but haven't done it by ourselves. As guys we become the type of men we are, not overnight, but as a result of our decisions, the choices we make, and those who surround and support us. And it is those people we need to thank.

To our teachers, thank you for sharing your talent and knowledge, and the occasional movie. What you did for us often went beyond the call of duty.

To our parents, thank you for supporting us in more ways than it's easy to reconcile. Not just this year past, but for the last 13 years of school.

To those sport coaches who provided us with strong counsel and guidance, thank you for making school about more than just classwork.

For the last five years I have been proud to be a student who attended Christchurch Boys' High School. And from today onwards for the rest of my life, I will be a proud Old Boy, giving back to those before me, as they have given to me.

Some of us will not cross paths again. Some of us will likely be seen on TV. Others in print. Some of us will also probably end up in prison. I have thoroughly enjoyed growing up with you all. It has been an honour and delight to share these years with you. I know that as I look out at all of you, I will measure my time here in the friendships I've enjoyed in these last years.

I don't know where it goes from here for any of us — for you, for anyone, and as sure as hell not for me. But I wish you the very best in your journey, and thank you for all being part of mine. Wherever we go and whatever we do, may we always be friends when we meet again.

* Senior Monitor = Head Prefect/Head Boy

Jake Bailey, 2015

2 FIRST IMPRESSIONS

Read the text through again.

Think: What does the speaker want us to think about/do/join/change, and so on?

Write down one thing we are being encouraged to do as a result of hearing this message.

The speaker wants us to _____

_____

_____ .

Unpacking the text

*In a non-fiction text, whether it be a persuasive piece or a speech, every paragraph contains an idea that relates to the overall purpose. Think about it like a jigsaw, in that each paragraph is a piece that connects to the pieces that come before and after. Looking at the individual pieces is what we call **unpacking the text**.*

1 FIND THE PATTERN

Look at each paragraph by itself and summarise the idea — the jigsaw piece — in one sentence. A few have been done for you as examples.

Paragraph	Summary
1	
2	
3	That this speech is a summary of the past.
4	
5	
6	You have worked hard to become men but haven't done it alone.
7	
8	
9	Thanks to coaches, as school is about more than the classroom.
10	
11	
12	Don't know what the future will bring but let's meet as friends.

It is okay if you write down similar ideas because often the author is repeating their idea in different ways to hammer home their point.

2 SUMMARISE

In no more than three sentences, write what this piece is about.

_____

_____

_____

_____

_____

_____

Complete the following sentence:

The writer/speaker wanted to teach us about _____ because

_____

_____.

Identifying how the idea is communicated

*Remember: ideas are communicated through a variety of **language features or language techniques** for a range of purposes.*

features = techniques

1 Fill in the blanks to show the various purposes:

- to _____ the reader
- to _____ a point
- to _____ words or ideas
- to _____ in the reader's mind (imagery)
- to _____ our thinking
- to _____ us to act (call to action).

2 The following language features can be found in the text. Find and label on the text (on page 76) an example of each of the techniques in the box below.

personal pronoun	listing	contrast
adjective	parallel structure	use of te reo Māori
repetition	metaphor	colloquialism

3 Fill in the following grid about the ideas in the text and what techniques help communicate these ideas. We have started it off for you.

Techniques	Explain the purpose of the technique	Evidence from text of the technique	Explain the effect
use of te reo Māori		'Tēnā koutou katoa'	Lets us know this is a formal occasion and that it is connected to New Zealand.
personal pronoun			Makes us feel that we are being spoken to directly and included in the speech.
parallel structure	Using the same pattern of speaking/writing to show ideas have equal importance.	'To our teachers, …' 'To our parents, …'	

Putting it all together

Now that you have spent some time 'unpacking' the text, recognising its language features, and thought about the effects, the meaning and the author's purpose, it's time to put all the parts together and practise writing the types of answers you will need to write in your examination. You can use the notes you have made in the previous pages to help you.

1 Select (✓) ONE language feature that sets the tone.

☐ listing ☐ metaphor ☐ colloquialism
☐ personal pronoun ☐ contrast ☐ adjective
☐ parallel structure ☐ use of te reo Māori ☐ repetition

2 Give an example from the text.

_____

_____

3 Explain how this and/or other language feature(s) help you **understand** the speaker's **attitude** towards **finishing high school**. You might consider:
- the speaker's feelings towards the topic
- the range of people mentioned in the speech
- the particular language features used.

We have included starter sentences for your paragraph. Complete each sentence thoroughly and you will have a great paragraph answer.

The speaker's overall purpose in this piece is to _____

_____

_____.

His attitude towards this topic is _____

_____

_____.

We see this attitude when the speaker uses the technique of _____

_____

when he writes [insert quote] '_____

_____,

_____.

The effect of this is to emphasise/highlight _____

_____

The reason for this is _____

_____

_____

_____

ISBN: 9780170415965 PHOTOCOPYING OF THIS PAGE IS RESTRICTED UNDER LAW

Another way this attitude is shown is through the technique of _____,

which we see in the line [insert different quote] ' _____
_____,
_____.

From this we learn _____
_____
_____.

It makes us think about _____
_____

in our own lives _____
_____
_____.

Finally, the author wanted us to remember/act/learn that _____
_____
_____

because _____
_____
_____
_____
_____.

ISBN: 9780170415965

NON-FICTION 3

Now that you have worked through two non-fiction texts, we will be starting to remove some of the activities. This doesn't mean that they are no longer important, but, rather, we are hoping that you are starting to work through them naturally yourself as you read the texts. Remember to pay attention to the language used, the context/background and your first impressions.

Pre-reading activities

1 VOCABULARY WORK

Match the correct term and definition in the grid below.

Term
housed
smoko
fidgety
unpredictable
compass

Definition
a rest period during work
not to be foreseen or foretold
contained
an instrument determining directions
restless; impatient; uneasy

2 After considering these definitions, what do you think might be the subject matter of the text?

I think the piece will be about _____

_____

because _____

_____ .

ISBN: 9780170415965

Reading the text

1 Read the extract through once, slowly (out loud if you can). Don't do anything else; just read.

A World of Books

I grew up in a home without books; no one read to me when I was a baby or when I was a child. I did not have a bookshelf in my room filled with books by Enid Blyton, Charles Dickens or Dr Seuss. In the living room, the bookshelf housed only an old *Bible*, a hundred-year-old text on veterinary science and horses, and volume one of *Reader's Digest Classic Adventure Stories*. The rest of the space was taken up by pot plants, photographs and empty coffee cups.

But, we children grew up in a world of story-tellers, surrounded by the voices of our elders who, often around the fireplace with someone strumming a guitar, would swap tales of people, places and things: what happened this afternoon, the other day, late last year or once upon a time.

My mother also filled our heads with stories: we would listen to her as she spoke on the phone, over the smoko in the shearing shed or in the car on our trips into town. She would paint us pictures with her words and, when I was old enough, I began to do the same.

I was nine years old and made to stay in bed with her and my newborn sister. Mum needed a rest and I was a fidgety and unpredictable child so she plonked me beside her in the double bed and shoved the Reader's Digest volume into my hands.

Bored with trying to sit still and quiet so as not to wake the baby, I turned to the first chapter of *Call of the Wild*. With a stubby finger, I picked out the individual letters and was surprised to see them swim together into recognisable words. The words joined the others on the page and within moments I had dived deep into the Alaskan wilderness: my mother, my sister and the hot afternoon gone.

Books quickly became my compass. They are the road map of my learning about my world. Reading, to me, is an adventure: I don't always know where I am going, how long my journey will take or what I will discover on the way. Now, I am the one who paints pictures for other people with my words and I live in a home filled with books.

By T.K. Roxborogh, author and playwright.
Adapted from http://www.vln.school.nz/groupcms/view/929002/tania-tk-roxborogh.

2 FIRST IMPRESSIONS

Read the text through again.
Think: What does the speaker want us to think about/do/join/change?
Write down one thing we are being encouraged to do as a result of hearing this message.

The writer wants us to _____

_____

_____.

ISBN: 9780170415965

Unpacking the text

*Remember, think about it like a jigsaw: looking at the individual pieces is what we call **unpacking the text**.*

1 FIND THE PATTERN

Look at each paragraph by itself and summarise the idea — the jigsaw piece — in one sentence. One has been done for you as an example.

Paragraph	Summary
1	
2	
3	
4	It was chance that gave the writer the book.
5	
6	

It is okay if you write down similar ideas because often the author is repeating their idea in different ways to hammer home their point.

2 SUMMARISE

In no more than three sentences, write what this piece is about.

_____

_____

_____

_____

_____

_____

Complete the following sentence:

The writer/speaker wanted to teach us about _____ because

_____

_____ .

ISBN: 9780170415965

Identifying how the idea is communicated

*Ideas are communicated through a variety of **language features or language techniques**.*

features = techniques

1   The following **language features** can be found in the text. Find and label on the text (on page 83) an example of each of the techniques in the box below.

personal pronoun	listing	colloquialism
parallel structure	adjective	personification
alliteration	metaphor	

2   Fill in the following grid about the ideas (purpose) in the text and what features are used to help communicate these ideas.

Language feature	Explain why writers use this technique	Evidence from text of the technique	Explain the effect
personal pronoun			
adjective			
colloquialism			
parallel structure			
listing			
metaphor			

Putting it all together

Now that you have spent some time 'unpacking' the text, recognising its language features, and thought about the effects, the meaning and the author's purpose, it's time to put all the parts together and practise writing the types of answers you will need to write in your examination. You can use the notes you have made in the previous pages to help you.

1 Select (✓) ONE language feature the author uses to describe their attitude towards reading.

☐ colloqualism   ☐ metaphor   ☐ listing

☐ personal pronoun   ☐ parallel structure   ☐ alliteration

☐ adjective   ☐ personification

2 Give an example from the text.

_____

_____

3 Explain how this and/or other language feature(s) help you to **understand** the writer's **attitude** towards **reading**. You might consider:

- the tone the piece is written in
- the image the writer is building in your mind
- the overall purpose of the piece.

Here are some **possible** sentence starters to help you.

The speaker's overall purpose in this piece is to …
Their attitude towards this topic is …
We see this attitude when the speaker uses the technique of … when he writes [insert quote] '…'
The effect of this is to emphasise/highlight …
The reason for this is …
Another way this attitude is shown is through the technique of …, which we see in the line
    [insert different quote] '…'
From this we learn …
It makes us think about … in our own lives …
Finally, the author wanted us to remember/act/learn that …
because … just like in the text when …

_____

_____

_____

_____

_____

_____

_____

_____

_____

_____

ISBN: 9780170415965

NON-FICTION 4

This is the final text in this section with some activities. Remember to pay particular attention to the language used, the title and the point of change.

Pre-reading activities

1 VOCABULARY WORK

Create a sentence with each of these words in it (their definitions are given in brackets).

a impending (about to happen, cannot be avoided)

_____

b tangible (real or actual, rather than being imaginary)

_____

c fabricated (devised or invented)

_____

d thrice (three times, in succession or quantity)

_____

e surmises (thinks or guesses without strong evidence)

_____

f impudent (insolent, rude, cheeky, immodest)

_____

2 TITLE

a The title of this non-fiction text is 'The Rude Question' and it was written by a Year 12 student. What question(s) would Year 12 students find rude?

_____

_____

b After considering the definitions and the title, what do you think might be the subject matter of the text?

I think the piece will be about _____

_____

because _____

_____.

ISBN: 9780170415965

Reading the text

1 Read the non-fiction piece through once, slowly (out loud if you can). Don't do anything else; just read.

The Rude Question

'What do you want to do when you grow up?' I don't know how many times I've been asked this question. I wouldn't have to care either, if it wasn't so rude. Over time it gets very frustrating that, as a teenager, I am just expected to know exactly how my career — and my whole life in general — is going to pan out. Sometimes it seems as if the older generation have forgotten what it's like to be young. Either that or they just don't care.

I have had to develop a range of different answers in an effort to satisfy the adult asking The Rude Question. The only problem is, there are no right answers — but plenty of wrong ones. For instance, I might tell the truth and simply state that I don't know what I want to do with my life. That is a very bad idea. The impending judgement is almost tangible; the adult obviously surmises that I must be totally unmotivated with no meaning or direction in my life whatsoever. In other words, my existence has no real purpose. If I simply say, however, that I want to keep my options open at the moment, the grown-up will usually play career counsellor and try to 'help' me come up with a job which I could do (usually it is something stupid I would never dream of doing in a million years). But obviously, I politely have to agree with them, and pretend I've now got my whole life sorted. Thanks to their constructive advice, of course! The worst one, though, is if I make up some random career simply to please the adult. I foolishly used to reserve this explanation for my parents' friends. I always thought it sort of got me off the hook, but I was wrong. Very wrong. Almost always, the parent-friend would quiz me ruthlessly on whichever random career idea I'd fabricated. That was *after* I'd heard all about their fourth cousin thrice removed on the second great-aunt's side who did that job which I had no desire whatsoever to pursue.

What I really hate, though, is that it is only really adolescents who get tortured with The Rude Question. Sure, a little kid may get asked what they want to be when they're bigger, but it is perfectly acceptable for them to say they want to become a nurse or a firefighter. Nobody actually expects them to have their whole life planned out. Nevertheless, when you become a teenager it is pretty much assumed that you know what you want to do and you are taking active steps to achieve it. It is sort of like you have to justify your existence.

I do wonder, though, how many adults, at the same age, knew what they wanted to do (and if they were correct!). Certainly, if I asked any adult what they wanted to do with their life (even if they hadn't really started any sort of job or career), I would be seen as being cheeky and quite impudent. So why is it, then, that adults feel that it is appropriate for them to ask me what I want to do with my life? In fact, I do think it is reasonably rude, and the expectations create a lot of additional pressure and stress for the future. Besides, even if I have got my whole life mapped out at the tender young age of sixteen, why should I have to share it with, more often than not, virtually a total stranger?

Of course, most people feel like there's nothing else to talk about with a teenager. So, naturally, they revert to asking The Rude Question. This really wouldn't be too bad, though, if they didn't have such high expectations of us. Certainly as young people we should be expected to do our best, but isn't it enough simply to be giving school our best shot, and trying hard at what actually does matter for us at the moment? Do we really need to be so certain of the future?

Maybe adults simply don't realise how hard it is to choose a career. Perhaps they don't understand the pressure on young people these days to do well. Whatever reason it is, though, it doesn't make The Rude Question any less rude. I think adults really ought to try putting themselves in our shoes.

Frania Cowie, Year 12, 2015.

2 FIRST IMPRESSIONS

Read the text through again.

Think: What does the speaker want us to think about/do/join/change?

Write down one thing we are being encouraged to do as a result of hearing this message.

The writer wants us to _____

_____

_____.

Unpacking the text

1 FIND THE PATTERN

Look at each paragraph by itself and summarise the idea — the jigsaw piece — in one sentence. One has been done for you as an example..

Paragraph	Summary
1	
2	That the narrator has had to invent answers to this question.
3	
4	
5	
6	

It is okay if you write down similar ideas because often the author is repeating their idea in different ways to hammer home their point.

2 SUMMARISE

Complete the following sentence:

The writer/speaker wanted to teach us about _____ because

_____

_____

_____.

ISBN: 9780170415965

Putting it all together

1 Select (✓) ONE language feature the author uses to express her feelings towards adults.

- [ ] rhetorical question
- [ ] short sentence
- [ ] alliteration
- [ ] adjective
- [ ] metaphor
- [ ] personal pronoun
- [ ] repetition
- [ ] compound word
- [ ] hyperbole

2 Give an example from the text.

_____

_____

3 Explain how this and/or other language feature(s) help you **understand** the writer's **attitude towards 'The Rude Question'**. You might consider:

- the writer's feelings towards adults
- what the writer thinks teenagers should worry about
- the overall message.

_____

_____

_____

_____

_____

_____

_____

_____

_____

_____

_____

_____

_____

_____

_____

_____

_____

_____

_____

_____

ISBN: 9780170415965

NON-FICTION 5

Using all of the skills you have been practising throughout this chapter, give this your best shot.

Put your timer on for 20 minutes. Read the piece, use your strategies and answer the questions. Good luck!

Ducks and Drakes

It is my day off so earlier today I drove out along the peninsula with a bag full of camera gear. I turned into the car park at Macandrew Bay, thinking that perhaps a leisurely coffee at a table overlooking the beach would be a good way to start taking photos, but I had to swerve to avoid a great knot of ducks writhing its way across the tarseal. A young female, small and exhausted, was struggling beneath a jostling mass of drakes, perhaps six or eight of them, who were all striving to copulate with her. They grasped her and climbed on her, pushing each other aside, not fighting but careless in their single-mindedness. I asked myself if I should intervene. Here was nature, red in tooth and claw, doing its normal everyday thing, and who am I to impose my anthropomorphistic* disgust on a perfectly natural phenomenon? My inner struggle lasted about as long as it took to put the car in neutral and turn it off. I opened my door and approached them. They were so intent that I got within an arm's length before they took notice of me. I could have reached out and banged a few heads together, but I clapped my own hands instead and they scattered, leaving the young female dazedly staggering across the car park. The drakes, some fully mature with their dazzling green heads, and some no older than the young duck, looked briefly at their forsaken prize, then at me, and flapped energetically off in all directions. The duck looked at me, her saviour, and recoiled in fear, flapping tired wings and rising crazily into the air, at about head height, flew straight past me and into the side of a passing truck. So much for intervention! There was a sickening thud and a tangle of feathers. She fell, dazed to the ground and lay there for a bit. One of the drakes returned and nuzzled her briefly and, slowly, she rose and walked at his side across the road and into the sea. She looked, from a distance, anyway, to be OK and they looked fairly well bonded. So why hadn't he fulfilled his part of the bonding agreement and protected her from what might have proven the injurious or even fatal attention of the others? Weak or stupid, I guess. Or maybe just as young and inexperienced as she was.

I had lost any taste for coffee. I had lost any taste for taking photos. I drove home aware of my own deep measure of disturbance, and thinking about why this bothered me so much. You don't have to look far for evidence of people behaving with as much self-interested disregard as those drakes, and, as often as not, justifying their cruelty with appeals to the naturalness and healthiness of their impulses.

Those drakes know no better. They are innocents. We do. We are not.

*anthropomorphistic: giving human form or attributes to an animal, plant, material, object, and so on.

By Kelvin Wright, retired Bishop of Dunedin.
From http://vendr.blogspot.co.nz/2016/10/ducks-and-drakes.html, retrieved 23 March 2017.

1 Select (✓) ONE language feature used to express the writer's feelings towards the drakes.

☐ rhetorical question   ☐ adjective   ☐ parallel structure

☐ short sentence   ☐ metaphor   ☐ onomatopoeia

☐ alliteration   ☐ personal pronoun

2 Give an example from the text.

_____

_____

3 Explain how this and/or other language feature(s) help you to **understand what disturbed** the writer and **why**.
You might consider:
- what the writer sees and hears
- how the writer's feelings change
- why the writer's feelings change.

_____

_____

_____

_____

_____

_____

_____

_____

_____

_____

_____

_____

_____

_____

_____

_____

_____

_____

_____

_____

_____

_____

Using all of the skills you have been practising throughout this chapter, give this your best shot.

Put your timer on for 20 minutes. Read the piece, use your strategies and answer the questions. Good luck!

Teenagers, or Seeds?

Teenage naivety. Did you feel that shiver run down your spine? The anxiety set in? These few uttered syllables are enough to make any parent's teeth set on edge. If a teenager sets one toe out of line, we are accused of being too 'innocent', and not understanding enough about the 'real world' to make our own decisions.

As teenagers, we haven't been exposed to a lot of things. I don't understand as much about mortgages and taxes as my parents, that's for sure. However, I think that the war against teenage naivety runs deeper than that. Our parents want us to understand that blind but blissful innocence can shelter you from the truth, and they want to tell us that truth. I'm sure some adults wish they had been told what to expect.

Maybe they all wish they had a warning of the responsibility they would have to accept. Maybe they think their role is to warn us, to give us the understanding they never had as teenagers. Maybe they want to protect us from the things we don't understand yet. It seems that a parent's biggest fear is that their teenager may make an uninformed decision. And I know that their warnings, their naggings and complaints, aren't done out of spite; they are done to protect us, to help us understand what we are getting into before we get too caught up in the moment.

But, the truth is, I don't want their warnings. I don't think everything can be so black and white; there are definitely far more shades of grey, especially when it comes to making decisions. I think there are some things that are just learned rather than taught. If you make a mistake, an uneducated decision, you learn, and you grow. We cannot be expected to grow up too fast. We are a generation of Peter Pans, no one wants to accept responsibility and adulthood before they have to, and we shouldn't have to.

I like to think of us teenagers as seeds. Small, and new in the world. If you give a seed a little bit of fertiliser, some water and sunlight, letting it grow in its own time, it will become a healthy and balanced plant. If you were to bury a seed in fertiliser, and keep it in the sunlight for too long, it may struggle to sprout. Both seedlings had the same potential, but one was forced to sprout before it was ready. It will become a small, sickly sapling. I think I know which seed I'd rather be.

Teenagers should be given the chance to learn in their own time. Just like the seed, we cannot be expected to grow up too fast. If we are buried in responsibility, and drowned in reality, we may not reach our full potential. I understand that moments of happiness are brief and fragile, but are they not still moments of happiness? Surely, a sip of joy is better than a glass full of cynicism? The truth hurts, and I have no doubt that we will discover that. However, I would much rather learn from my own mistakes than the second-hand mistakes of my parents.

Mess up, make bad choices. Understand what went wrong. Then, learn; grow, and be yourself. Live your own life, not the life someone else wants you to live, sooner than you want to live it.

Elin Harris, Year 12, 2015.

ISBN: 9780170415965   PHOTOCOPYING OF THIS PAGE IS RESTRICTED UNDER LAW.

1 Select (✓) ONE language feature used to express the narrator's feelings towards adults.

☐ rhetorical question	☐ adjective	☐ repetition
☐ short sentence	☐ metaphor	☐ listing
☐ alliteration	☐ personal pronoun	☐ imperative

2 Give an example from the text.

_____

_____

3 Explain how this and/or other language feature(s) help you to **understand** the writer's **attitude** towards **being a teenager**. Support your points with specific reference to the text. You might consider:

- the writer's overall opinion
- why the writer has chosen to express her opinion this way
- the overall message.

_____

_____

_____

_____

_____

_____

_____

_____

_____

_____

_____

_____

_____

_____

_____

_____

_____

_____

_____

_____

abridged   (of a book, film, poem, etc.) shortened, without losing the main sense of it.

adjective   a word that describes the noun. For example: hot, cold, blue, big, small.

adverb   a word that describes the verb (how or when or where the action is done). For example: He smiled **sadly**. They were **nowhere**. **Yesterday**, I went to the park.

alliteration   the repetition of consonant sounds. For example: **T**iny **T**im **t**rod on **D**on's **t**oes. (The 'd' is also alliteration.)

allusion   a reference to another literary or well-known work or person. For example: I was no Shakespeare but I loved writing plays.

anecdote   a story used to illustrate an idea. For example: When I was a small child …

assonance   the deliberate repetition of the same vowel sound followed by a different consonant sound. For example: A st**i**tch **i**n t**i**me saves n**i**ne. The 'i' sound in 'stitich' and 'in' are the same; the 'i' sound in 'time' and 'nine' are the same.

attitude   the opinion, point of view, type of behaviour of a person about a topic, person or thing.

book-ending   phrases and/or ideas placed at the beginning and at the end of a passage.

cliché   an over-used expression. For example: It was a dark and stormy night.

colloquialism   informal language, usually spoken. For example: Howzit going, bro?

compound word   two or more words are joined together to form a new word; sometimes joined with a hyphen (-). For example: babysitter, mother-in-law, homegrown.

conjunction   a word that joins two sentences together. For example: and, but, so, because, therefore.

connotation   something suggested or implied by an object or thing. For example: Black cats always make me nervous.

contrast   the use of words or images that are opposite in likeness. For example: I was feeling hot and cold all night.

convincing   including more than one example to support what you are saying and explain what you mean (magic 'because').

direct address   when the narrator is speaking directly to the reader. For example: I'm interested in *your* thoughts on global warming.

euphemism   a nicer way of saying something that is usually unpleasant or unkind. For example: He was 'let go' (fired). She's under the weather (sick).

extended metaphor   a metaphor is used and then multiple comparisons are added to develop the image.

extract   a passage or part taken from a book or article.

facts/statistics   numbers and specific examples used to support an argument. For example: Around 65% of statistics are made up. She's worked here for 18 years so knows what is going on.

fiction   made-up stories to entertain, persuade and/or teach a moral.

hyperbole   an exaggeration. For example: I'm so tired I could sleep for a month.

imagery   used to communicate visually an idea and/or create a mood.

imperative/command   an order or command for an action. For example: Don't hit your sister.

incomplete sentence   a sentence without a verb and or a subject. For example: Unfortunately for them. After the rain.

infer   hint, imply, suggest.

jargon   specialised language used by people who work together or share a common interest. For example: Getting **endorsement** for all **subjects** is good, but you still need to have **Level 2 Literacy** for **University Entrance**.

ISBN: 9780170415965   PHOTOCOPYING OF THIS PAGE IS RESTRICTED UNDER LAW.

juxtaposition   the deliberate placing of two things side by side by comparison or contrast. For example: We invited both our friends and our enemies.

listing   related words or phrases arranged as a list. For example: I eat toast, cereal and a banana for breakfast.

literal   strict meaning, true to fact, not exaggerated.

magic 'because'   'because' is a magic word, as it forces us to explain or justify our statements.

metaphor   a comparison between two things where one thing is said to be another. For example: The playground **is a jungle**. All the students **are wild animals**.

narrator   the person or character who is telling the version of events/story.

non-fiction   a piece of writing based on facts and reality or offering an opinion. For example: biography, autobiography, textbook, letter to the editor, speech.

onomatopoeia   the sound of the word imitates or suggests the meaning or noise of the action described. For example: crash, gurgle.

parallel construction/structure   repeating the same word class order in close succession, e.g. proper noun + adjective + verb + preposition + noun. For example: 'It was the best of times; it was the worst of times' (*A Tale of Two Cities*, Charles Dickens).

perceptive   making links between the ideas in the text and your observation of the wider contexts (either the fictional world of the text or the real world).

personal pronoun   words that stand in place of proper nouns. For example: he, she, me, you, I, we, us, them, they.

personification   when a non-living thing is given living characteristics or when a non-human thing is given human characteristics. For example: The lift groaned on the way down.

phrase   a sequence of two or more words working together as a single image or idea. For example: a broken down rust heap.

preposition   a word used to show the position of a thing in relation to another thing. For example: on, above, behind, inside, under.

pun   an expression that plays on different meanings of the same word or phrase. For example: I've been to the dentist so many times, I know the drill.

quotation   direct use of another's words, either spoken or written. For example: As the principal reminds us, 'To lead, you must serve.'

repetition   words or statements used more than once for effect. For example: The room was cold. Too cold to think.

rhetorical question   a question to which no answer is required. Used for dramatic effect. For example: Who knows?

rhyme   the repetition of words with similar sounds. For example: There was an old horse from Cant**ucket**, who ate from a rusted brown b**ucket**.

rhythm   the beat or pattern of stresses that occur in poetry and music and often used for effect in prose.

short sentences   one- to three-word sentences, often phrases. For example: Try it. Now.

show understanding   explain your statements in terms of the meanings and effects created.

sibilance   repetition of 's' sounds in two or more words; often used to indicate a sinister event or feeling. For example: The **s**lippery **s**nake **s**lithered acro**ss** the gra**ss**.

simile   a phrase that compares two things, using 'like', 'as' or 'than'. For example: They behave **like** monkeys in the classroom, but are **as well behaved as** royalty in the playground.

stanza   a grouping of lines in a poem similar to verses in a song.

symbol   an image/picture that represents an idea. For example: A dove represents peace.

tone   the overall impression of the author's attitude towards a topic, event or character. For example: humorous, sad, happy, peaceful.

use of punctuation   the deliberate use of the comma or exclamation mark or ellipsis or other punctuation marks for effect.

use of te reo Māori   using Māori words, expression — often without immediate translation. For example: Kia ora, friends, I send my aroha to you.

verb   a doing word. For example: I **ate** my lunch, then **walked** to class.

ISBN: 9780170XXXXXX

ANSWERS

You will find some sample answers to the activities here. Many of the questions do not have one correct response so if you get a different answer to us, don't assume you are wrong. Think about why we wrote *that* answer and why you wrote *your* answer. Talk to someone else about *their* answer. Discussing how and why you came to a response is another excellence skill to learning how to get familiar with unfamiliar texts. Most of the time in English analysis, provided you can support it with clear examples and explanations, your answer is correct for *your* reading of the text. We have written paragraph-type 'answers' for the final questions for each text. The last two NCEA practice exercises have some annotations to show you the distinction between Achieved, Merit, and Excellence level responses. The phrases and sentences in orange indicate Merit-level commentary (convincing); the phrases and sentences in blue indicate Excellence-level responses (perceptive).

NARRATIVE PROSE

NARRATIVE PROSE 1: Friendly Persuasion

Pre-reading activities, pages 7–8

1   Possible answers:
   b   My cousin was **expelled** from the swimming club.
   c   I can be **persuaded** to come to the movies if you pay for me.
   d   We've moved to Christchurch because my mum was **transferred** from her job in Auckland.
   e   The **atmosphere** in the dance club is like a crowded sauna.
   f   The army gathered up all the weapons in its **armament** to see what was still needed.
   g   When my sister doesn't get her way, she always puts on a **pouting** face of unhappiness.
   h   My uncle has four **apprentices** working for his plumbing business.
   i   Like knights of the round table, George was arrogant and **cavalier** in nature.
   j   **Holy orders**, unlike promises, are made between you and God and are forever binding.
2   a   Friendly: behaving in a kind, benevolent, helpful manner towards others.
      Someone who is always happy and chatty and seems to enjoy being around people.
      Persuasion: the act of persuading or prevailing upon someone to do something by advising or urging them.
      Being really good at being able to convince someone to agree with your ideas.
   b   I think the story might be about a well-liked person who is really nice and has to get her friends to agree to help her do something because the word friendly makes me think of a nice, happy person and the word persuasion means convincing others to do something, so I think the story will have a character convince their friends to do something for them.
3   Some of the words we associate with 'school': *assignments, NCEA, tuck shop, friends, classrooms, teachers, assemblies, smelly rooms, exams, after-school detention, bells, crowded buses, mufti days, athletics, sports.*

Reading the text, pages 9–10

2–4 Check with a classmate, your teacher or your parent/guardian.

Using the 'Three Level Reading Guide', page 11

1   Level One: **a** False **b** True **c** True **d** False
   Level Two and Level Three: All of these answers can be true or false because it depends on your intrepretation (so long as you can explain why you think it is true/false).
2   Share your answer with a classmate, your teacher or your parent/guardian.

Identifying the 'point of change', page 12

1   Paragraph 7: 'Alan, when he received the summons …'
2   The story no longer describes all the funny and naughty things Alan gets up to. The principal/school won't tolerate him any more and he is kicked out.

ISBN: 9780170XXXXX   PHOTOCOPYING OF THIS PAGE IS RESTRICTED UNDER LAW.

3 The school failed to change Alan's behaviour so they got rid of him just like the previous school. Alan hasn't learnt anything — he carried on behaving like he always had and the consequence for him was that he got rejected — again. If we don't learn from our mistakes, we will keep making them and keep getting rejected by people.

Using the title to help you understand the author's purpose, page 12

1 Alan is a friendly student and tries to use his charm to get people to give him what he wants. The word 'persuasion' is a good word too as it's a nicer (and friendly) way of making people do something they may not want to do.

2 Everyone is trying to keep Alan happy, which the author thinks is a bad thing because Alan never has to face consquences — his parents are weak and he (and the principal) is able to tell them what to do instead of them being in charge of their kid like parents are supposed to do. The author believes bad things eventually happen to kids of parents who don't teach boundaries and consequences to their kids.

3 Share your answer with a classmate, your teacher or your parent/guardian.

4 The title and the point of change work together to get across the author's purpose that we need to take responsibility for our actions. They do this because the words Friendly Persuasion mean that no one is trying very hard to get Alan to change his behaviour, and when it gets bad at the point of change in the text, the schools just pass him on. We all need to learn to take responsibility for our actions. Children need to be taught this (by their parents) and modelled it (by adults). If they don't learn this, bad things can and will happen, like Alan dying when he crashes his car.

Identifying how the text is communicated, page 13

1 See list of examples in 'Putting it all together'.

2 Share your answer with a classmate, your teacher or your parent/guardian.

3 inherited: the school had to take Alan because he was kicked out of his other school

persuaded: they were told what to do

people's best interests: everybody agreed they didn't want Alan because he was a bad student

he naturally didn't intend to do any work himself: he was lazy

an incident: there was a fight

were invited along: they had to go to the meeting

received the summons: Alan was in a lot of trouble and the principal was very angry

pointed in the direction of the gate: he was kicked out of school

proper ratbags: really naughty

after his departure: after being kicked out of school

unrecognisable: he was killed and his body so badly burnt, no one could tell who it was

Putting it all together, pages 14–15

1–2

adjective:	disastrous, (fairly) crackling, giggly, redhead, blonde, little, charming, irresponsible, cheerful, slim, tanned, black-haired, hazel-eyed, happy
listing:	slim, tanned, black-haired and hazel-eyed
question:	What would the Principal suggest? … Did the Principal know that they'd just bought Alan a second-hand Mini as a birthday present?
metaphor:	locked in mortal combat; armament
repetition:	totally charming … totally irresponsible; to others … those others; suggest … suggestion
euphemism:	invited along; … incident
alliteration:	whispering to a little redhead. On Wednesday
compound word:	black-haired, hazel-eyed, second-hand
contrast:	The girls all wanted to mother him; the boys all wanted to smother him

3 The author, David Hill, wanted to highlight the issue of *what happens when parents do not teach their children to take responsibility for their actions* because *when students behave badly and get away with it, they often hurt others and/or themselves*. He does this by using the technique of *metaphor* when he writes *'blonde and redhead were suddenly locked in mortal combat'*. This is effective because *it uses war imagery to describe how serious the conflict between the students was and to emphasis how serious (and bad) things were between the students after Alan behaved irresponsibly toward the two girls*. Another technique the author uses is *simile*, for example when he says *'became responsible and mature, as they did in all the best stories'*. This means *the author expects that there will be a good ending for Alan despite his silly behaviour* and is used to emphasis the idea that *by contrasting what actually happens — there is no happy ending for Alan because he dies*. This makes us think about *the negative consequences for students and schools when parents do not take responsibility for teaching their children the right way to behave* so that we *do as teenagers understand why our parents (and teachers) sometimes don't let us have our own way*. Finally, the author wanted us *to remember that we there are ALWAYS consequences for the things that we do* because *by remembering this important life lesson, we might stop and think before we make a poor decision*, just like in the story when *Alan's parents let him go off in the car when he is supposed to be grounded. By not making Alan deal with the consequences of his bad behaviour, he loses his life.*

NARRATIVE PROSE 2: from *Four Letters of Love*

Pre-reading activities, pages 16–17

1
a	civil servant	someone employed by the government
b	severity	harshness or sternness
c	wiry	resembling wire, lean and sinewy
d	angular	consisting of an angle; bony, lean and gaunt
e	fewness	being small in quantity
f	frailty	having delicate health; weak
g	emerges	to come into view from being concealed

Words that you would associate with 'father' and 'God' — answers will vary.

2
Four	A cardinal number
Letters	Written or printed communication
Of	Used to indicate origin or source
Love	Tender and passionate affection for someone

3 Words that you would associate with 'Ireland' or 'Irish' — answers will vary.

Things about Greystones: It is a coastal town; It is named after the stones between two beaches; It is close to Dublin (the capital of Ireland); It was put on the map in 1855 with the building of the railway.

Reading the text, pages 17–20

2 a The narrator is male.

b The tone is cold/unfeeling

c The text is going to be about the narrator's father becoming a painter.

4 b *Thin* — 'tall and wiry, with bones poking out of his skin'; 'high frailty'; 'ribcage and shoulders like a twisted jumble of coathangers in an empty suit bag'; 'my father is thin as air'; 'wave ... might snap him like a wafer'; 'angular figure'

Tall — 'tall and wiry'; 'high frailty'

Grey hair — 'his hair had turned silver'

Blue eyes — 'dazzling blueness of his eyes'

Wearing a suit or a cardigan — 'my father in a grey suit'; 'changes into a cardigan'

c See list of examples in 'Putting it all together'.

5 The narrator *focuses on the physical description because* he wants to build an image in our mind of what his father looks like. For example, the constant references to his father's thinness emphasises this and creates a believable image in our mind. *What is missing* is any description of what the father is like as a person — is he kind, funny, thoughtful? We would normally describe people with the physical and personality traits.

6 What can we infer from this focus on physical description that the boy and his father do not have a close relationship? The boy doesn't know how to describe his father as a person, only as a thing. Although they are together doing things, such as at the beach, they are always apart — the dad is swimming while the boy holds the towel. They don't actually do activities together.

7 Check your answer with a classmate, your teacher or your parent/guardian.

Using the 'Three Level Reading Guide', pages 20–21

1 Level One **a** True **b** False **c** True **d** False

Level Two: **a** True **b** True

Rest of the answers for Level Two and Level Three can be true or false because it depends on your interpretation (so long as you can explain why you think it is true/false).

2 Share your answer with a classmate, your teacher or your parent/guardian.

Identifying the 'point of change', page 21

1 Paragraph 3

2 We see a change in paragraph 3 as the narrator stops describing his father and instead talks about his painting. We see a change because of the words the author chooses to use: 'My mother ... admired his talent then' and the narrator 'noted with a small boy's pride the small WC that was his mark.' These lines show a foreboding of what is to come, that things were positive for the family at the start when the father started painting but we know it doesn't end well, as his wife and son are no longer proud of him.

Identifying how the text is communicated, page 22

1 See list of examples in 'Putting it all together'.

2–4 Share your answers with a classmate, your teacher or your parent/guardian.

Putting it all together, pages 22–23

1–2
adjective:	civil, thin, tall, wiry, silver, age, severity, touched, dazzling, blueness, fewness, little, grey, great, frozen, high, frailty, twisted, jumble, empty, invisible, pale, naked, blue-grey, early
listing:	He was a thin man, tall and wiry
simile:	shoulders like a twisted jumble of coat hangers; My father is thin as air; it might snap him like a wafer

ISBN: 9780170XXXXX   PHOTOCOPYING OF THIS PAGE IS RESTRICTED UNDER LAW.

metaphor:	The great shelf of his forehead; The words have vanished; dressing himself into the New Year
repetition:	off the stones, off the ends; as he stands, moment he stands ... Still, he stands
personification:	The words have vanished; the briefcase flopping by the telephone table
alliteration:	**h**is **h**air **h**ad; kit**ch**en ... **ch**anges; **c**ardigan ... **c**omes; shelf o**f** his **f**orehead **f**loating; a high **w**ave crashes across his **w**ading things it might snap him like a **w**afer
compound word:	twenty-four, blue-grey
assonance:	bl**ue**ness of his **ey**es and the f**ew**ness; h**a**ve v**a**nished and I **a**m

3 The narrator describes his father as someone who *is a quiet, strange man without obvious physical strength*. We see this description when Williams uses the technique of *simile* when he writes *'his ribcage and shoulders like a twisted jumble of coat hangers'*. The effect of this is to *highlight his thinness by comparing his body to something man-made, wiry, and not 'natural' looking or normal. The reason for this is to remind us that the narrator's memory of his father is of a person who does not look like the other fathers he saw as a child. The reason for this is because he is linking this image to the disturbing idea that his father heard from God.* Another way this attitude towards his father is shown is through the way his appearance is described using the technique of *metaphor*, which we see in the text where is says *'The great shelf of his forehead floating'*. From this we learn *that a dominant memory for the narrator is of the father having a large forehead. It makes us think about the image of a shelf also and a place where valuable objects are put up out of reach of children because they are dangerous or too good to be touched by children, which creates a sense of mystery. The fact that the narrator describes the father only in physical terms and not emotional ones suggests that though the father was a physical presence in his life, they did not connect emotionally. This means that they did not have a close emotional bond.* It makes us think about *our own relationship with our parents because it forces us to think about whether we have a deep or superficial relationship with them.* The author wanted us to realise that *children need to feel like they know their parents as an individual, not just what they look and act like.*

NARRATIVE PROSE 3: from *The Crimson Petal and the White*
Reading the text, pages 24–25
2–3 Answers will vary. Check your answer with a classmate, your teacher or your parent/guardian.
4 **a** **Sight:** complete darkness; unlit houses; ashen hour of night; blacking-grey; haze of my own spent breath; air is frigid; **Sound/hearing:** muffled drunken voices; **Touch/feel:** air is bitterly cold; uneven ground; blinking against an icy wind; grip you so tightly; sleet stings your cheeks; feel hot; ears being to hurt; cobblestones ... wet and mucky; **Smell:** smells of sour spirits; dissolving dung
  b touch/feel — could argue that it is sight
  c By using the sensation of touch/feel the most frequently in this extract, Faber makes us feel like we are there as we can really imagine what the cold feels like. He uses words that help transport us to the dark, cold night.

Identifying the 'point of change', page 26
2 Paragraph 3
3 The effect of 'And yet you did not choose me blindly' is that it forces us to become involved in what the book is saying and to acknowledge that the book is talking directly to us.
4 'Instead, you find yourself hoping to God that the voices come no closer.'
5 This line changes our perception of the book in that it makes it sound quite scary and like we are in danger.
6 keep your wits about you; you have not been here before; you are an alien; you find yourself recognising nothing; you've allowed yourself to be led astray and it's too late to turn back now.
  The author's purpose is to let us know this isn't just another book about Victorian London, but that this book will show you a different, and more true, side of London and to be prepared.

Identifying how the text is communicated, page 27
1 See list of examples in 'Putting it all together'.
2 Check your answers with a classmate, your teacher or your parent/guardian. Some suggestions follow:

Technique	Example	Effect
adjective	This city I am bringing you to is **vast** and **intricate**	The choice of these two words emphasise how large the city of London is and how it is complicated both physically and socially.
simile	Sharp little spits of it so cold they feel hot, **like** fiery cinders in the wind	This comparison builds an image in our mind, which includes the sensation of touch. It helps us feel like we are really there, experiencing this bitter cold.
imperative	Watch your step	Creates a sense of urgency and danger for the reader.
alliteration	smells of sour spirits and slowly dissolving dung	The repeated 's' sound in this emphasises the unpleasant smells being described.

3 The tone is one of warning and instruction.
4 The effect of this tone is to create a sense of danger and urgency for the reader. We also feel like we have no choice in what is happening, as the book is telling us what is happening and where we are going and that it is 'too late to turn back now.'

Putting it all together, pages 28–29

1–2

adjective:	vast, intricate, well, bitterly, cold, complete, darkness, uneven, icy, unknown, unlit, full, coy, good, fast, sharp, little, cold, hot, fiery, late, ashen, blacking-grey, undisturbed, burnt, haze, wet, mucky, frigid, sour, muffled, drunken, grand, romantic, nothing, warm, simple, right
imperative:	Watch your step; Keep your wits about you; Let's not be coy
simile:	they feel hot, like fiery cinders in the wind; readable like undisturbed pages of burnt manuscript; doesn't sound like the carefully chosen opening speeches of a grand romantic drama
metaphor:	you are an alien from another time; I first caught your eye; make yourself at home
repetition:	connections ... Connections; Unknown street ... unlit houses ... unknown people
personal pronoun:	You, I, they, your, me
alliteration:	hesitate, still holding; Sleet stings your cheeks; sharp little spits
rhetorical question:	Why did I bring you here? Why this delay ...?
personification:	those stories flattered you; welcoming you as a friend; treating you as if you belonged; Sleet stings your cheeks; sharp little spits; the voices come no closer

3 The narrator is describing London as a dangerous, unfriendly place because he wants the reader to feel unsettled and uncertain. We see this when the author uses the techniques of imperative when he writes 'watch your step. Keep your wits about you'. The effect of this is to emphasise the possibility that the reader may get hurt or lost. The reason for this is to make the reader rely on the narrator to help navigate the way through the story. Another way the idea of the negative attitude towards the city of London is shown is through the multiple use of negative adjectives such as 'bitterly', 'cold', 'darkness', black', etc., which contribute to the feeling of London being an unpleasant place, as all these words have horrible connotations and by including lots of them, it emphasises all the bad aspects of the city. By describing London in this awful way, the narrator forces the reader to depend on 'him' for a safe passage through the streets. The author is personifying the purpose of a narrator of a story because when we read a story, sometimes we forget that the 'telling' of the story is through a narrator and that we are dependent on that narrator for giving us our impressions of characters, place and action. By addressing the reader directly, the author is reminding us of this convention that we are dependent on the narrator to gain safe passage through the events of the story.

NARRATIVE PROSE 4: Red Pen

Reading the text, pages 30–31

2 Answers will vary. Share them with a classmate, your teacher or your parent/guardian.

3 Red: blood; love; warning; danger; stop; incorrect
Pen: tool; creation; fixing; correcting

4 Answers will vary — some suggestions follow.

a This story is about a boy who is struggling to write a story in a silent classroom. The narrator isn't struggling with the task as much but she understands the boy and wishes she could help him.

b **i** He isn't very good at writing. **ii** He doesn't care about school. **iii** He has a lot of pressure on him.

c **i** She likes the boy. **ii** She would rather be at home. **iii** She likes writing.

d They are friends and she cares about him.

Identifying how the text is communicated, page 32

1 See list of examples in 'Putting it all together'.

2 Check your answers with a classmate, your teacher or your parent/guardian. Some suggestions follow.

Technique	Example	Effect
metaphor	Words bear down on him	It helps us understand the pressure (the weight) the boy feels at having to complete the writing task assigned to him.
simile	There's this silence ... Like fog	We can visualise that the silence is lingering around and creating a barrier between the narrator and the boy.
onomatopoeia	rustles; ruffling; scribble	These words allow us to create a vivid image in our mind of what the writer is describing.

3 The effect of present tense is that it makes us feel like we are there, right now, as this is happening. We also want to reach out and help the boy with his writing.

Putting it all together, page 33

1–2

adjective:	broken, hollow, blank, dull, nicer, well-mannered, red, fallen, lost, new, exhausted, vast, empty, messy, awful, quiet, bright, blue, few
listing:	dropping in, ruffling my hair, leaving again
simile:	silence ... like fog; it spreads on and on like a vast desert; farther than the desk that separates us
metaphor:	only a shadow of what he once was; there's a distance that's farther than just the space between our chairs
repetition:	alone but not lonely; slightly; maybe
onomatopoeia:	rustling, rustle, coughs

ISBN: 9780170XXXXX   PHOTOCOPYING OF THIS PAGE IS RESTRICTED UNDER LAW.

alliteration:	**s**hrug **s**lightly; try to give him a **s**oft, **s**lightly for**c**ed, **s**mile but he'**s** not looking; **p**ick up ... **p**en ... empty **p**age; **b**lue lines **b**lurring ... **b**right **b**lue
personification:	words bear down on him; inspiration is not with him today; silence hanging around the classroom; my ears try to breathe it in; where the quiet is nicer, well-mannered; it welcomes me in; the breeze ... dropping in, ruffling my hair; mocking him with blue lines
compound word:	well-mannered, despair-filled

3 The narrator feels sorry for the boy and how difficult he is finding the writing task during class time. We see this with the descriptions associated with the boy such as the adjectives 'broken', 'hollow', 'blank', 'dull', 'empty'. These negative words build up a negative and unproductive picture of how the narrator thinks the boy is feeling about writing because of the association of these words. These contrast with the positive adjectives used to describe what writing is like for the narrator when at home when she uses positive adjectives like 'nicer', 'well-mannered' and personification of the concept of quiet as being welcoming. The reason for this is to suggest that trying to be creative in a classroom is very difficult for some students — even the narrator, who seems to find writing easier than the boy. This idea of the difference between them is shown in the simile of them being 'farther than the desk that separates us'. However, the narrator does not give up on the boy because she thinks that it is not that he is unskilled at writing a story, but rather the setting is having a negative effect on him. The writer is wanting to challenge us, especially teachers, to consider that sometimes our true abilities are not made obvious because of the wrong circumstances — just like the boy in this story with no inspiration in the uncomfortable classroom setting and who is already set up to fail because he only has a red pen to do his writing — a symbol to represent what teachers use to mark student work, often identifying parts that are wrong.

NARRATIVE PROSE 5: from *Third Degree*
Pages 34–35
1–2

adjective:	well, peeling, funny, plastic, nasty, dead, childish, new, small, tight, free, busting, shy, shamed, cruel, unhappy
listing:	horses, and dogs and clouds and a funny man; pick and jab, and pull and tug; pinch, pull, tug, wipe
simile:	hangs in strips just like my skin
metaphor:	I have decorated the walls with my mind; I am busting
repetition:	Lie still. Lie still!; Jab, jab, jab, wipe, jab, jab, jab, wipe; look ... look ... looking; The hands jump ... It jumps for me because I cannot jump; feeling shy, feeling shamed
parallel structure:	my brother comes to visit me ... my mother comes to visit me; feeling shy, feeling shamed
alliteration:	**p**eeling **p**aint; **h**ut in the **h**aybarn; with my **f**ace, on my **f**orehead; **s**he **s**mells of **s**oap; **b**ack with **b**lood
personification:	tweezers with nasty ridges of teeth; the mask suck in and out with her breathing; the instrument stabs me; It jumps for me because I cannot jump
incomplete sentence:	Looking at him standing near the window, looking out; Jab, jab, jab, wipe, jab, jab, jab, wipe.

3

Answers the question and **shows understanding** of how the narrator feels about being in hospital **ACHIEVED**	The author wants us to understand how isolated, lonely and frightening being in hospital is for the narrator. She does this by using the metaphor 'I have decorated the walls with my mind'. 'Decorated' is a happy, positive word and is often associated with celebrations. This makes the actual situation Ruth is in even more bleak: there is nothing to be celebrated here as she is severely injured. Also, there are no posters or child-friendly pictures around the hospital room. Yet, despite her injuries, the child narrator is able to use her imagination to brighten the dreary room — changing 'peeling paint' into objects like 'unicorns and a funny man'. By repeating the phrase 'Lie still', the author is reminding us that, unnaturally, the burned child cannot move so must spend her energies taking in her surroundings: describing what she sees ('the peeling paint'), using negative adjectives associated with the nurse ('cruel', 'tight', 'unhappy'). The narrator also personifies the clock when she says 'it jumps for me because I cannot jump' in the same way a frightened or traumatised child might transfer their feelings onto a toy or another object to speak on its behalf. The movement of the clock's hands are highlighted because she cannot move, as well as acting on behalf of a child who can't move (or speak).
MERIT answer *plus* Explains author's purpose and makes insightful links to world and shows perceptive understanding **EXCELLENCE**	Also, repeating the phrase 'jab, jab, jab' highlights the painful and monotonous treatment the narrator must endure, thus reminding the reader that despite the 'shapes in the peeling paint', the narrator is unable to escape her situation and must put up with the unsympathetic and unhelpful attitude of the nurse. The purpose of this is to emphasise the resilience of children — their strong spirits. The idea that even during something truly awful, children can see positive things. In the same way we see Syrian refugee children playing games in the camps or singing nursery rhymes, the narrator's natural curiosity and heightened imagination gives us hope that children can recover from trauma.

Convincing because provides more explanation and detail *plus* more examples and discussion provided *equals* MERIT

NARRATIVE PROSE 6: Beach Patrol
Pages 36–37

1–2

adjective:	proper, dumb, discarded, half, tall, muscly, mean, quick, rude, hard, ugly, high, worried, serious, wide, shocked, intelligent, sickening, satisfying
listing:	RTD bottles, crisp packets and someone's underpants; tall, muscly and mean
simile:	rammed into the sand like military sentinels; pushed back arms and shoulders like a gorilla
metaphor:	half filled with their droppings; Robbie hovered just behind me; high-tailing it off the beach
repetition:	dumb … dumbness … dumb-ass; hard shove … falling hard
onomatopoeia:	groaned, moaned, barked, clicked
alliteration:	**S**ea Cadet**s s**ervice book; **s**ummer … **s**natched the **s**eed **s**ack; **B**aldy … **b**arf
colloquialism:	get lost, mates, kid, scram, nah, barf, man, cops, dumb-ass, stuff, their gear, give us a hand
compound word:	saving-foolish-swimmers, out-of-towners, shaved-headed, finger-printing, dumb-ass, high-tailing

3

<table>
<tr>
<td>

Answers the question and shows **understanding** of how the narrator feels about being in hospital
ACHIEVED

</td>
<td rowspan="2">

The narrator does not like the surfers because they are littering the beach. We know this because of the negative way the surfers and their actions are described. The writer lists objects that are particularly disgusting bits of rubbish out of place on a beach, such as glass 'RTD bottles, crisp packets and someone's underpants'. The effect of this list of strange objects makes the littering more disgusting for the reader and helps us to be sympathetic to the narrator because he has to pick up these things left by the older boys. He also uses negative adjectives such as 'dumb', 'mean', 'rude', 'ugly' when talking about the surfers to emphasise not only the behaviour of the surfers but the narrator's attitude towards them. The reason for this description is to highlight how stupid the narrator thinks these surfers are because they are not taking care of the environment, which the narrator thinks is unwise because we are polluting our beaches and seas and killing off our marine life. He also uses a simile to describe the actions of one of the surfers as being 'dumb' when he says 'pushed back arms and shoulders like a gorilla'. For most people, the gorilla is a less developed species than humans, and often describing someone as a gorilla or a monkey is to say they are dumber than intelligent humans; in other words, not picking up your rubbish is foolish because we will all suffer from a polluted planet. Despite the risk of getting hurt, the narrator confronts the two surfers because he believes strongly in taking care of our environment. The author communicates this using humour and colloquial language ('nah', 'man', 'stuff', 'cops') so that although we find the exchange funny between the brothers and the surfers, we can understand the message because we can imagine this actually happening because this is how kids talk. It makes us consider how we might behave if we see people polluting the beach, challenging them like the narrator and Robbie do.

</td>
</tr>
<tr>
<td>

Convincing because provides a number of details and explanation **(He also uses …, He also uses …, The author communicates …)**
MERIT

</td>
</tr>
</table>

Blue provides explanation of author's purpose and makes insightful links to world and shows perceptive understanding **EXCELLENCE**

POETRY

POETRY 1: My Sister's Top
Pre-reading activities, pages 38–39

1 **a** emblem — a sign or design that represents something
   b reminiscent — awakens memories of something similar
   c papyrus — an ancient document written on material made of this plant, very fragile
   d blotch — a large, irregular spot
   e lavender — a pale, bluish purple

2 **a** Sister's: something belonging to a female sibling/a female sibling is something
   my sister is the focus
   Top: the name for a piece of clothing worn as a shirt or T-shirt/the best at something
   thinking about the T-shirts I have, especially my second-hand ones; who is always the best at something

   b Share your answer with a classmate, your teacher or your parent/guardian.

3 Share your answer with a classmate, your teacher or your parent/guardian.

Reading the poem, page 40

2–3 Check with a classmate, your teacher or your parent/guardian.

ISBN: 9780170703XXXXX   PHOTOCOPYING OF THIS PAGE IS RESTRICTED UNDER LAW.

Using the 'Three Level Reading Guide', page 41

1   Level One: **a** True **b** False **c** False **d** False **e** True
    Level Two and Level Three: All of these answers can be true or false because it depends on *your* intrepretation (so long as you can explain why you think it is true/false).

2   Share your answer with a classmate, your teacher or your parent/guardian.

Identifying the 'point of change', page 42

1   Line 10, 'Still'

2   A detailed description of the top.

3   A description of the connection between the top, the poet, and her sister.

4   Share your answer with a classmate, your teacher or your parent/guardian.
    The close study of the top evokes memories for the poet and perhaps makes her miss her sister and/or the (good) times she had when her sister was wearing the top that is now the poet's.

Linking the title with the end of the poem, page 42

1   My Sister's Top; then gave it to me.

2   EITHER *the sister gives the poet 'hand-me-downs/discarded/unwanted clothes, which might show the sister doesn't value the relationship with the poet OR the sister giving her top to the poet is a gift, which means that they have a close bond.*

Identifying how the poem is communicated, page 43

Share your list of ideas and the effect and/or purpose of the examples you choose with a classmate, your teacher or your parent/guardian. Here are our ideas:

What idea?	Technique	Evidence	Explain the effect and/or purpose
The top is old and stained	noun	'blotch'	'blotch' means uneven, a mistake; the word helps to describe what the top looks like.
The top reminds the poet of her sister	adjective	'reminiscent'	A word used to explain how an object evokes a memory.
They have been to some fun childhood holidays	alliteration	'Mickey Mouse'	Draws attention to the name, which is a famous Disney character associated with fun times.
The poet enjoys wearing the top	simile	'soft as an animal's fur'	This is a pleasant description and emphasises how pleasant the associations the poet has for the top (and her sister).
The poet likes the top	metaphor	'floating in a sea of cream'	The top brings up images of comfort and gentleness because of the word 'floating', which makes you think of resting on something else, freely and easily, and the sea of cream, where cream is thick and yummy.

Putting it all together, pages 44–45

1–2

adjective:	lavender, blue, soft
personal pronoun:	me, she
simile:	soft as an animal's fur
metaphor:	island of paint; floating in a sea of cream
rhyme:	sea of cream
alliteration:	**b**lue **b**lotch; **M**ickey **M**ouse; **s**urrounded ... **s**trip ... **S**till ... **is** reminis**c**ent ... **s**ister ... time**s s**he

3   The poet is saying that even though the top is old and stained, she feels *positive* towards her sister's gift. We see this attitude when the poet uses the technique of *simile* when she writes *'soft as an animal's fur'*. The effect of this is to emphasise/highlight *that the top is cherished like a beloved pet.* The reason for this is *to make us think about the comfort we get when we stroke the fur of a pet and to link this feeling to how the poet feels about her sister's top and her sister.* Another way this attitude is shown is through the use of *the metaphor*, which we see in the text where it says *'floating in a sea of cream'*. From this we learn *that the top brings up images of comfort and gentleness because of the word 'floating', which makes you think of resting on something else, freely and easily, and the 'sea of cream', where cream is thick and yummy.* It makes us think about *the idea that in our own lives, even though family members can leave our house, because of how we often link clothes and smells to them, they are never far from our minds.* It makes us think about *how even though family members can leave our house, because of how we often link clothes and smells to them, they are never far from our minds.* Finally, the poet wanted us to remember that *we can be connected to our siblings from something as simple as 'hand me down' clothes because of all the memories associated with the object. Just like in the poem when the poet says that the hand-me-down top reminds her of her sister.*

POETRY 2: Invigilator

Pre-reading activities, page 46

1
agitated:	moved or stirred up
think tank:	a group of people who think of new ideas on a particular subject
wharf post:	part of a structure to which boats are tied to, immovable and permanent
back wash:	a backward flow or movement produced especially by a propelling force
navigate:	to find the way to get to a place when you are traveling
kelp:	a mass of large seaweeds

2 a The word has a greater responsibility — more like a rule keeper.

b Directing or producing a film or a television show, making sure eveyone does their allocated jobs; a marshal in a running race or horse eventing competition, making sure no rules are broken and that everyone has the same opportunities.

3 Share your answer with a classmate, your teacher or your parent/guardian.

Reading the poem, pages 47–48

2-3 Check with a classmate, your teacher or your parent/guardian.

Using the 'Three Level Reading Guide', pages 48–49

1 Level One: **a** True **b** False **c** True **d** False

Level Two and Level Three: All of these answers can be true or false because it depends on *your* intrepretation (so long as you can explain why you think it is true/false).

2 Share your answer with a classmate, your teacher or your parent/guardian.

Identifying the 'point of change', page 49

1 Line 19, 'all together now'

2 There is a somewhat negative tone describing students going into and then sitting their exam and being anxious and isolated/alone in their task.

3 A sense of relief/freedom/joy.

4 Share your answer with a classmate, your teacher or your parent/guardian.

The students unite in their joy that they 'survived' the exam experience, 'the miraculous force', and leave the assembly hall, 'vanish', as one group.

Identifying how the poem is communicated, pages 50–51

1 See list of examples in 'Putting it all together', but here are our ideas.

Term	Example	Effect
metaphor	students flood the assembly hall	lots of students/too many/uncontrolled/a bit frightening
alliteration	it's a thin**k** tan**k**	Hard sounds of the 't' and 'k' like knocking or tapping the head, like someone trying to get their brain to work
metaphor	I'm a wharf post	old, weather beaten, been around for a long time, immovable despite all the movement of the tides coming and going/students sitting exams every year
assonance	d**e**nse w**e**t	emphasis of these two words amplifies how wet, how heavy; negative connotations
pun	fish rise from the deep … force of your schooling.	draws attention to the image and makes us think that students act like brainless fish, pushed and swayed by the tides (or their schooling/education)
cliché	hear a pin drop	we all know the meaning of this overused phrase, that it means so quiet
personification/ metaphor	the names glitter	like stars/stand out/in contrast to the idea of them all being like each other (school of fish moving in the same way)

2 a-e Share your list of ideas and the effect and/or purpose of the examples you choose with a classmate, your teacher or your parent/guardian.

Putting it all together, pages 52-53

1-2
adjective:	curved, green, agitates, dense, wet, together, deep, miraculous
assonance:	**a**nd **a**gitated h**a**nds n**a**vigate the ex**a**m; d**e**nse w**e**t
use of punctuation:	no capital letters, no punctuation points
metaphor:	students flood; hands navigate; I'm a wharf post … back wash; light of assessment; force of your schooling
pun:	schooling; think tank
cliché:	hear a pin drop
alliteration:	thin**k** tan**k**
personal pronoun:	I'm

ISBN: 9780170703XXXXX   PHOTOCOPYING OF THIS PAGE IS RESTRICTED UNDER LAW.

3   The poet is saying that her experience of the exam is *unpleasant*. *To her, the whole experience of sitting examinations is like all the hard things about being at sea.* We see this attitude when the poet uses the technique of *a metaphor* when she writes 'agitated hands navigate the exam'. The effect of this is to emphasise/highlight *how fast the students are moving their hands to answer the questions*. The reason for this is *to show the stress the students are under. The word 'agitate' shows stress and worry and if you are trying to steer a boat (navigate) and you're not very good at it, then you could hurt yourself or capsize/sink. The description of the hands being agitated indicates that the students do not feel prepared well enough and are worried they might do badly.* Another way this experience is shown is through the technique of *a cliché*, which we see in the line *'hear a pin drop'*. From this we learn how *quiet it is in the room because we all know the familiar phrase, which emphasises also how on edge the students might be. It makes us think about our own exam experiences in our own lives and to understand that the act of sitting examinations is something difficult for most people. Even though we cannot see how others are coping in the exam, the narrator sees everyone and sees everyone is stressed.* Finally, the poet wanted us to remember/act/learn that *sitting examinations is not going to go on forever* because *there is light at the end* just like in the poem when *the poet uses the positive words of 'glitter' and 'vanish' to show that we can 'swim away' like the schools of fish do.*

POETRY 3: Tooth, page 54
Reading the poem, pages 54–55
2-3 Answers will vary. Check with a classmate, your teacher or your parent/guardian.
4 Answers will vary but should be along the lines of how the poet is saying that with her tooth knocked out, her daughter seems younger and that the fall has transported her back in time.

Identifying the 'point of change', pages 56–57
1 Line 10/11
2 Line 21/22
3 Relaxed and happy
4 fossick; wave; float; polished
5 Sad and hurt
6 As I stroke you; your eyes collect water; your gums are an ocean of blood; a tear-drop's caress
7 Hopeful; resigned

Identifying how the poem is communicated, pages 56–57
1 See list of examples in 'Putting it all together'.
2 Answers will vary — some suggestions below.

Feature	Example	Effect
alliteration	**T**oday, you're **t**welve **t**eeth old	Makes the sentence stand out in our mind so we pay attention to it and remember it.
direct address	As I stroke you	Makes us feel like we are there, that we are the ones who have lost a tooth and are getting a cuddle.
listing	Shells, starfish, pipi and paua	Lets us know how many different things are scattered along the beach and builds a specific image in our mind. The use of te reo Māori also lets us know this poem is set in New Zealand.
metaphor	Your gums are an ocean of blood	This exaggeration of how much blood is caused by the loss of the tooth allows us to imagine how much shock and pain the child is in and how it can feel overwhelming.

4 The loss of the tooth.
5 It helps the reader understand the process of the loss of the tooth because the poet wants us to experience this with her. She compares it to boating because it shows how things can be calm, then rough, and then calm again, so that we might think about how when things like this happen in our own lives.

Putting it all together, page 57
1-2
alliteration: **T**oday, you're **t**welve **t**eeth old; **p**ipi and **p**aua; **w**hen **we w**ave; re**s**t **s**afely upon it**s s**tarboard
metaphor: your eyes collect water; your gums are an ocean of blood; a tooth anchored to blue; tooth's a boat isolated by low tide
adjective: polished, deep, blue, woollen, old, younger, white, hull-shaped, isolated
personal pronoun: you're, we, you, your
listing: we fossick for shells, star-fish, pipi and paua
simile: and have grown, like Lazarus, younger beneath moonlight
direct address: I'll show you how it can rest safely
extended metaphor: All the boat and water references: tide goes out; yachts moored in the marina; float along; keel over; ocean of blood; anchored; tooth's a boat
personification: a tear-drop's caress

ISBN: 9780170415965

3 The poet, Siobhan Harvey, starts the account of the day in the poem positively so that the event of losing the tooth is more shocking. She does this by including personal pronouns, which allow us to feel that we, too, are experiencing the nice day at the marina. Examples 'we fossick for shells' and 'we wave goodbye to yachts moored in the marina' mean that this is a shared, positive experience. Also, the pronoun and direct address of 'you' in the phrase 'you keel over' makes the reader feel as if they are the one who has suddenly fallen over. The poet uses these metaphors and personal pronouns to help us understand her shock at her child losing her tooth. By saying that 'your eyes collect water; your gums are an ocean of blood', we can imagine the shock of this fall and the pain of the tooth being knocked out because the imagery exaggerates how much the child cries and how it seems that there is a lot of blood, especially after such a lovely day. The combination of the two techniques allows the reader to experience the sudden loss of this tooth the same way the poet did, in shock. We may even remember the time it happened to us — losing a tooth this way. However, the poet recovers quickly, and uses the extended sailing metaphor to express how she can show us (the reader) 'in the morning' how the tooth can 'rest safely on its starboard'. She does this to assure herself (and her child and us) that though bad things can and do happen, it is not the end of the world and to be encouraged that there will be always be a new day with new experiences.

POETRY 4: If We Return, page 59
Reading the poem, pages 59–61
2 Answers will vary, but some suggestions: sad; confused; excited; wondered what they were fighting for; missed their friends; surprised to see women doing roles that men traditionally did; amazed that things could just be the same.

3
a	liberty	freedom from (external or despotic) control
b	blossom	the state of flowering
c	agony	extreme and prolonged pain
d	carelessly	unconsidered
e	guardians	people who guards protect or preserve
f	earn	to get in return for labour or service

4 Answers will vary. Check with a classmate, your teacher or your parent/guardian.

Identifying the 'point of change', page 61
1 Line 10

2 The poet is asking if England will still be the same place when the soldiers return, a place to work 'earn our bread' and live.

3 Answers will vary, but it could be: sad; resigned; questioning. Any line from the first nine lines can be used as evidence, as long as it makes sense with the identified tone.

4–5 Answers will vary, but could be: negative; resigned; weary; guilty; depressed. Any phrase can count as evidence, as long as it makes sense with the identified tone.

Identifying how the poem is communicated, pages 62–63
1 See list of examples in 'Putting it all together'.

2 Some suggestions follow:

Langage feature	Example	Effect
rhyme	Be/me; bread/dead	The rhyme scheme means that the poem flows nicely when read and it is pleasant to say and easy to remember. This is the opposite of the negative tone of the poem and serious concept it is tackling.
rhetorical question	If we return, will England be/ Just England still, to you and me?	Makes us stop and question what it must have been like for the survivors of the war. We usually only consider that they are lucky to have come home, not the repercussions of living in a changed world and with the memories of what they did and saw.
repetition	If we return; England; dread	This repetition of 'If we return' hammers home to us the uncertainty of surviving war. The repetition of 'England' lets us know which country is being returned to and fought for. The repetition of 'dread' lets us know that it is not with joy that these men returned.

Putting it all together, pages 62–63
1–2
alliteration: If **w**e return, **w**ill England; **w**e **w**ho have **w**alked ... and **w**atched
metaphor: smile of agony
adjective: blood-guiltily, red
personal pronoun: you, me
repetition: If we return; dread
rhyme: be/me; bread/dead; Liberty/carelessly; red/shed
rhetorical question: If we return, will England be/Just England still to you and me?/The place where we must earn our bread?
personification: English fields shall blossom red

3 The poet, F.W. Harvey, describes England as a place that will feel different when the soldiers return after war. He feels a sense of uncertainty and uses a rhetorical question, combined with personal pronouns ('If we return, will England be/Just England still to you and me?') to make the reader to think about the answers themselves and to realise that it wasn't a simple matter of surviving the war and returning home. The reader feels like the question is directed right at them, and for the first time, they have to consider the long-term effects of what is seen in war, on those that survived. This is reinforced by the technique of adjective when Harvey describes us as holding 'blood-guiltily/The things that men have died to free'. The negative words of 'blood' and 'guiltily' are contrasted with the idea of those who have died so that the survivors are able to be 'free'. This is an acknowledgement of survivor guilt, which is an affliction suffered by those who go through a traumatic event such as war or a natural disaster — like an earthquake — but survive where friends or others did not. It is also an acknowledgement that soldiers who have been to war might have had to kill people to survive. The poet is asking us to think about the truth that to return to England, and be free, we had to kill. And these same men that died alongside or opposite us were also fighting for freedom. By repeating the phrase 'If we return' emphases the risk going to war has — not everyone does come back but, 'If' they do, they will be changed. The poet is communicating their idea that even if you survived physically unscathed, you will not be uninjured and that returning to England will be no simple matter because you will be changed by your war experience.

POETRY 5: Morning
Pages 64–65

onomatopoeia:	buzzing, splash
adjective:	swale, dip, notorious, many-pointed, best, light, cold, early, steaming, heavy
personal pronoun:	we, his
simile:	the lawn steaming like a horse in the early morning
rhetorical question:	Why do we bother with the rest of the day ...?
repetition:	buzzing around the house on espresso
personification:	then night with his notorious perfumes; the typewriter waiting
parallel structure:	and buzzing around the house on espresso ... but mostly buzzing around the house on espresso

3

> Answers the question and **shows understanding** of how the narrator feels about the morning **ACHIEVED**

> MERIT answer *plus* Explains author's purpose and makes insightful links to world and shows perceptive understanding **EXCELLENCE**

The poet, Billy Collins, loves the morning. He starts the poem with a rhetorical question 'Why do we bother with the rest of the day ...?', which sets us up from the start to think about which part of the day we like best. The word 'bother' also lets us know how he thinks negatively about the rest of the day. This is a biased attitude and by including us, there is an expectation that we agree with him that 'mornings' are the only part of the day worthy of attention. He then uses adjectives to emphasise how he feels about the other parts of day, the 'swale' of the afternoon and 'dip' into evening. These words could both be seen as having negative connotations, therefore contrasting with his positivity about the morning with the positive adjectives of 'best' and 'early'. This is then further emphasised through the use of 'buzzing around the house on espresso'. This is also a positive image, and one that many readers can relate to because we all know that coffee wakes you up and gives you energy. The fact it is repeated, and used as part of a parallel structure, hammers home this happy image of someone's description of the morning. The poet is encouraging us all to get up early and put our energies into appreciating the mornings like him rather than lying in bed until much later and missing the best part of the day.

> **Convincing** because provides a number of details and explanation **(he then uses ..., This is then further emphasised ...)** **MERIT**

POETRY 6: A Work of Artifice
Page 66–67

1–2

adjective:	attractive, tall, side, high, small, cosy, domestic, weak, lucky, little, early, bound, crippled
onomatopoeia:	lightning, croons, whittles
listing:	small and cosy, domestic and weak
personal pronoun:	he, your, you
personification:	It [being the tree] is your nature/to be small and cosy,/domestic and weak
parallel structure:	the bound feet, the crippled brain, the hair in curlers
contrast:	could have grown eighty feet tall ... It is nine inches high
allusion:	the bound feet; the crippled brain; the hair in curlers; the hands you love to touch

Answers the question and **shows understanding** of the narrator's attitude towards the gardener **ACHIEVED**

MERIT answer *plus* Explains author's purpose of warning us to be careful of people who stunt our growth and makes insightful links to world and shows perceptive understanding **EXCELLENCE**

The poet, Marge Piercy, believes that the gardener is stunting the possible growth of the bonsai tree. We see this through adjectives and the use of contrast. We are told the tree is in an 'attractive pot' and it is 'nine inches high' but that it 'could have grown eighty feet tall'. We get a feeling straightaway that Piercy would rather the tree was eighty feet tall. The 'gardener croons' to the tree that it should be 'small' and 'weak'. These are adjectives with negative connotations, so again, we get the feeling that the gardener is doing something wrong. This is then made clear towards the end of the poem, where Piercy states that with living creatures we must 'begin very early to dwarf their growth', and she uses parallel structure to compare ancient cultural practices to attain beauty, which are no longer regarded as humane: 'the bound feet' with 'the hair in curlers'. This allows the reader to understand that the bonsai tree, which is being pruned and having its growth dwarfed by the gardener, is actually a metaphor for females and that the gardener is society. Most people think small things, like animals, or bonsais, are cute and are like pets to be controlled. We are therefore challenged to be alert to the 'gardener' who might be using soft and seductive noises to trick us into being compliant and contained rather than reaching for the heights we are capable of. The gardener and the bonsai alert us to the artificial (artifice) nature of what is happening — in the same way society tries to control and contain women so that they become a stunted version of themselves and not real.

Convincing because provides a number of details and explanation **(so again ..., This is then made clear ..., she uses ...)** MERIT

NON-FICTION

NON-FICTION 1: At Ten Years Old

Pre-reading activities, pages 68–69

1
a	scooter	a child's 'vehicle' with two wheels with a low foot-bed between them, steered by a handlebar
b	intricate	having many interrelated parts; complex; complicated
c	fete	a festive celebration
d	incomprehensible	impossible to understand
e	estimated	formed an educated opinion
f	recruited	raised (a force) by enlistment/force
g	invaluable	beyond calculable value
h	denied	withheld something from someone
i	campaign	a systematic course (often aggressive) for a particular purpose

2–3 Check with a classmate, your teacher or your parent/guardian.

Reading the text, page 70

2 Share your answer with a classmate, your teacher or your parent/guardian.

Unpacking the text, page 71

1

Paragraph	Summary
1	Memories of things the narrator did as a child, list of what Juliet lost when she was 10.
2	Comparing face painting at a fete with getting ready for battle.
3	Comparing music at home to the drum beat of battle troops.
4	List of the narrator's happy experience of play fighting, list of Juliet's experiences of war.
5	Tells us that Juliet isn't the only child to have had her childhood ruined.
6	Speaker tells us that she wants us to be more aware.
7	Speaker asks us to donate to Child Soldiers International.

2 Share your answer with a classmate, your teacher or your parent/guardian.

Identifying how the text is communicated, page 72

1 See list of examples in 'Putting it all together'.
2 Share your list of ideas and the effect and/or purpose of the examples you choose with a classmate, your teacher or your parent/guardian. Here are our ideas.

ISBN: 9780170415965

Techniques	Explain the purpose of the technique	Evidence from text of the technique	Explain the effect
statistics	This makes the argument more convincing and believable.	'300,000 child soldiers are estimated to be in combat as we speak, and another 500,000 are recruited'	As readers, we are appalled at the numbers of children being forced to go to war.
personal pronoun	To make the narrative personal to the author and the reader/listener.	'my', 'I', 'you'	We can't avoid the truth of the speech that we are being asked to be involved by either donating time or money or putting ourselves in Juliet's shoes.
listing	Adds weight to any argument by providing lots of examples to support points.	'against her will, from her family, from her friends, her education, school, and community'	The examples build up so that we feel not one aspect of Juliet's life was unaffected by the war.
parallel structure	Used to highlight differences in the subject matter of two or more sentences, using the same pattern of speaking/writing to show ideas have equal importance.	'I remember building mud huts … Juliet remembers building mud forts.'	Though they are the same in some aspects (age and gender), this structure highlights the differences and makes us even more appalled at what Juliet's life has been like.
repetition	To draw attention to the word/phrase.	child/childhood/children	By reminding us that we are talking about children/a child, the content of war and soldiers feels more awful because our association with childhood is one of innocence.
imperative	To compel the reader/listener to act a certain way/do something.	'make the time to donate'	Because it is a command, we feel like we have no choice but to act now.

Putting it all together, pages 73–74

1–2

statistics: 300,000 child soldiers; 500,000 are recruited

listing: against her will, from her family, from her friends; education, school, and community; mud huts … play-fighting … water fights, water ballons, and laughter

parallel structure: At ten years old … At ten years old …; I remember … I remember … Juliet remembers

anecdote: my days were filled; having my face painted; building mud huts, and play-fighting

jargon: campaign; child soldiers; combat; recruited; war; battle; grenades

contrast: At ten years old my days … At ten years old Juliet was …; my face painted by a senior student … painting her face with thick black tiger stripes; play-fighting … real fighting

repetition: At ten years old; child/childhood/children

personal pronoun: my, I, you

imperative: make the time to donate

3 The speaker's overall purpose in this piece is to *draw attention to the plight of child soldiers.* Their attitude towards this topic is *that they are being forced to live an unnatural life.* We see this attitude when the speaker uses the technique of *contrast in how she organises her speech into pairs of paragraphs. She compares her memories of being 10 with Juliet's memories. We see this when she says 'At ten years old I remember having my face painted … at our local fete. At ten years old Juliet remembers painting her face … for battle'. The effect of this is to emphasise the difference between the childhoods experienced by the girls.* The reason for this is because Addison wanted to point out that these children are not allowed to do normal childhood things, and they are being forced to grow up quickly, and do terrible things because the speaker wants us to do something to help these children. Another way this attitude is shown is through the technique of *connotations,* which we see in the *words 'denied', 'forced', 'slipped', which she uses to describe Juliet's situation. From this we learn that this is a terrible thing that is happening and that '300, 000 child soldiers are estimated to be in combat as we speak'. It makes us think about how lucky we are to experience peace in our own lives and how we should value the freedom we have, to enjoy a childhood. Finally, the author wanted us to act and to donate to Child Soldiers International because this is one of the ways in which we can help these children possibly experience the childhood that was stolen from them just like in the text when Juliet is forced to paint her face ready for battle.*

NON-FICTION 2: Head Boy's Prizegiving Speech
Pre-reading activities, pages 75–76

1–3 Check with a classmate, your teacher or your parent/guardian.

Reading the text, pages 76–77

2 Share your answer with a classmate, your teacher or your parent/guardian.

Unpacking the text, pages 77–78

1

Paragraph	Summary
1	He has cancer.
2	He shouldn't be alive to be here tonight.
3	That this speech is a summary of the past.
4	Formal greeting and introduction.
5	Thank you for supporting me.
6	You have worked hard to become men, but haven't done it alone.
7	Thanks to teachers for going beyond.
8	Thanks to parents for support.
9	Thanks to coaches, as school is about more than the classroom.
10	Proud to be part of the school now and in the future.
11	We don't know what the future holds, but I will measure the past in friendships.
12	Don't know what the future will bring, but let's meet as friends.

2 Share your answer with a classmate, your teacher or your parent/guardian.

Identifying how the idea is communicated, pages 78–79

1 • to **include** the reader
  • to **emphasise** a point
  • to **highlight** words or ideas
  • to **create a picture** in the reader's mind (imagery)
  • to **challenge** our thinking
  • to **encourage** us to act (call to action)

2 See list of examples in 'Putting it all together'.

3 Share your list of ideas and the effect and/or purpose of the examples you choose with a classmate, your teacher or your parent/guardian. Here are our ideas.

Techniques	Explain the purpose of the technique	Evidence from text of the technique	Explain the effect
use of te reo Māori	To be inclusive and recognise that Aotearoa/New Zealand is a bilingual nation.	'Tēnā koutou katoa'	Lets us know this is a formal occasion and also that it is connected to New Zealand.
personal pronoun	To make the narrative personal to the author and the reader/listener.	'I', 'we', 'us', 'you', 'they'	Makes us feel that we are being spoken to directly and included in the speech.
parallel structure	Using the same pattern of speaking/writing to show ideas have equal importance.	'To our teachers … To our parents'	This emphasises that the students have not done all the work (and gained their successes) on their own.
listing	Adds weight to any argument by providing lots of examples to support points.	'results of our decision, the choices we make, and those who surround and support us …'	The examples build up so that the listeners feel not one thing alone contributed to the experiences the students have had at school.
metaphor	Used to create an image in the mind of readers/listeners so that they have a clearer understanding of the point being made.	'call of duty'	This is a military term and reminds us that, like soldiers called up to fight in a battle or to help others, it is expected of all those in a regiment to do their share of serving others.
adjective	Used to describe in more detail certain objects and people and situations to help the reader/listener have a clearer understanding of what is being described.	'amazing'	The speaker uses the strong adjective of 'amazing' to describe the year just gone.

ISBN: 9780170703XXXXX

Putting it all together, pages 80–81

1-2

personal pronoun:	I, we, us, you, they
listing:	results of our decision, the choices we make, and those who surround and support us
contrast:	short and long
adjective:	amazing, new, fine, young, short, long, few, easy, strong, proud, best
parallel structure:	to our teachers … to our parents … to those sport coaches
use of te reo Māori:	Tēnā koutou katoa
repetition:	some of us; fine young men
metaphor:	call of duty; not cross paths; measure my time
colloquialism:	guys; sure as hell

3 The speaker's overall purpose in this piece is *to communicate how he and the other students have become men now they have finished high school and to thank those who have helped him.* His attitude towards this topic is *one of gratitude and a feeling of success.* We see this attitude when the speaker uses the technique of *parallel structure* when he writes *'to our teachers … to our parents … to those sport coaches …'* The effect of this is to *emphasise that the students 'haven't done it by ourselves'.* The reason for this is *that Bailey wants to highlight that who you become is a result of your own decisions and also those 'who surround and support us'.* Another way this attitude is shown is through the technique of *repetition,* which we see when he says *'I have been proud …' and 'I will be a proud …'*

From this we learn *that, although eager to leave, he will remember school with fondness and pride. Because of his recent diagnosis of cancer — 'you'll be dead in three weeks' — Bailey doesn't know what the future holds for him.* It makes us think about *the unknown* in our own lives because *he wanted us to think about how we should make the most of the time that we are given.* Finally, the author wanted us to learn that *we should thank those that have helped us, and to make sure that 'we always be friends when we meet again.' This is a great message for everyone, but particularly teenagers* because *sometimes we can hold on to grudges that are based on small things. His constant use of personal pronouns, 'I wish you the very best if your journey' makes it seem like he is speaking directly to each and everyone of us. This means that we take the message personally and will make sure we treat people in kindness (as friends) and with gratitude.*

NON-FICTION 3: A World of Books
Pre-reading activities, page 82

1

housed	contained
smoko	a rest period during work (often when a cigarette was smoked)
fidgety	restless; impatient; uneasy
unpredictable	not to be foreseen or foretold
compass	an instrument determining directions

2 Share with a classmate, your teacher or your parent/guardian.

Reading the text, page 83
2 Share with a classmate, your teacher or your parent/guardian.

Unpacking the text, page 84

Paragraph	Summary
1	Where the author grew up, there were no books in the home.
2	People around the author were storytellers.
3	The mother in particular told her lots of stories and when she was old enough, the author told stories too.
4	It was chance that gave the writer the book.
5	This was the moment the author realised she could read.
6	Books help the author understand the world.

2 Share with a classmate, your teacher or your parent/guardian.

Identifying how the text is communicated, page 85
1 See list of examples in 'Putting it all together'.
2 Share your list of ideas and the effect and/or purpose of the examples you choose with a classmate, your teacher or your parent/guardian. Here are our ideas:

Techniques	Explain the purpose of the technique	Evidence from text of the technique	Explain the effect
personal pronoun	To make the narrative personal to the author and the reader/listener.	'I', 'my', 'me'	To emphasise that this account is personal to the author — it is her story and her family experience and therefore unique.
adjective	Used to describe in more detail certain objects and people and situations to help the reader/listener have a clearer understanding of what is being described.	'filled', 'empty'	The author actually uses a positive word ('filled') to say that her world was empty of books — like the 'empty' ashtrays on the bookshelf.
colloquialism	By using informal language, the author/speaker is able to appeal to the reader/listener.	'smoko'	This is a rural New Zealand word and used to describe the rest time when workers would stop for a break. Emphasises that the writer's family are labourers rather than professionals, who would more likely take a 'tea break'.
parallel structure	Using the same pattern of speaking/writing to show ideas have equal importance.	'when I was a baby ... when I was a child'	Highlights the passing of time but that nothing had changed in terms of books being available until this moment.
listing	Adds weight to any argument by providing lots of examples to support points.	'Enid Blyton, Charles Dickens or Dr Seuss'	These are all traditional and famous writers, mostly for children, and the list is used to emphasis what was lacking in the writer's childhood. One would expect a child to have at least *one* of these authors' books.
metaphor	Used to create an image in the mind of readers/listeners so that they have a clearer understanding of the point being made.	'paint us pictures with her words'	This visual image is used to show that words have the power to create images (pictures) in our head — the mother did not provide books but she did provide stories and so the writer was still able to 'see' the pictures.

Putting it all together, pages 86–87

1–2

colloquialism: smoko

metaphor: filled out heads with stories; paint us pictures with her words; see them swim together; books became my compass; they are the road map of my learning; reading ... is an adventure; now I paint pictures for other people with my words.

listing: Enid Blyton, Charles Dickens or Dr Seuss; an old Bible, a hundred-year-old text ... and volume one of; tales of people, places and things; pot plants, photographs and empty coffee cups; this afternoon, the other day, late last year, and once upon a time; my mother, my sister and the hot afternoon

personal pronoun: I, my, we, our, me

parallel structure: when I was a baby ... when I was a child

alliteration: pot plants, photographs and empty coffee cups; smoko in the shearing shed; trips into town

adjective: filled, empty, bored; still; newborn, stubby, individual, recognisable, deep, hot, long

personification: the words joined the others on the page

3 The writer's attitude towards reading is a positive one. She didn't grow up with books and she tells us that 'no one read to me when I was a baby'. She states that she came across reading by accident when her mother 'shoved the Reader's Digest volume into my hands'. The connotations of the word 'shoved' are negative and makes us think that the mother was in a hurry or frustrated. She certainly didn't intend for the writer to get anything significant out of the book. However, the alliteration and imagery used in the phrase 'within moments I had dived deep into the Alaskan wilderness' make us realise that this was a turning point for her and how she was transported to another place. After this experience, 'books quickly became my compass', so this was a life-changing event. The writer wanted us to realise that sometimes it is the unintentional, and unexpected, things that change our lives. The writer uses parallel structure (sometimes known as book ending) to show us how this moment changed her life: 'I grew up in a home without books ... Now, I live in a home filled with books.' We are all aware that being read to as a young child is important, but what the writer wanted us to realise is that just because it didn't happen, doesn't mean that you won't be able to read and enjoy it, or, as the writer did, take the next step and become a writer yourself. This is a fantastic message, as it teaches the reader that things can come along at any point in our lives and change it for the better. Although we are shaped by our childhood experiences, we don't need to be defined by them.

NON-FICTION 4: The Rude Question

Pre-reading activities, page 88

1–2 Answers will vary. Check them with a classmate, your teacher or your parent/guardian.

Reading the text, pages 89–90

Answers will vary. Check them with a classmate, your teacher or your parent/guardian.

ISBN: 9780170703XXXXX   PHOTOCOPYING OF THIS PAGE IS RESTRICTED UNDER LAW.

Unpacking the text, page 90

1

Paragraph	Summary
1	How teenagers are always asked what they are going to do when they grow up.
2	That the narrator has had to invent answers to this question.
3	That it is only teenagers who are faced with this question.
4	That adults probably didn't know themselves when they were teenagers.
5	That adults can't think of anything else to ask a teenager.
6	That the question shouldn't be asked and adults should be more empathetic.

2 The writer/speaker wanted to teach us about how to talk to teenagers because she finds that she is always asked the same question and she finds this rude. The question puts a lot of pressure on the teenager and she believes that there is no right answer.

Putting it all together, page 91

1–2

rhetorical question: So why is it ... ask me what I want to do with my life?; ... why should I ... a total stranger?; ... what actually does matter for us at the moment?; Do we really need to be so certain of the future?

adjective: rude, frustrating, whole, older, young, right, range, different, wrong, bad, unmotivated, real, open, stupid, worst, constructive, random, correct, cheeky, impudent, best, certain, hard

repetition: rude; adults

short sentence: Either that or they just don't care; That is a very bad idea.

metaphor: get me off the hook; whole life mapped out; putting themselves in our shoes; giving school our best shot

hyperbole: a million years; adolescents who get tortured; fourth cousin thrice removed on the second great-aunt's side

compound word: parent-friend; great-aunt; grown-up

alliteration: **c**areer **c**ounsellor; **c**onstru**c**tive advice of **c**ourse

personal pronoun: you; I; my; me; we

3 The author clearly feels negatively towards the question that adults often ask teenagers, 'What do you want to be when you grow up?' The fact the author has used the adjective 'rude' from the start when defining this question sets this piece up to have a negative tone. This is emphasised throughout the text with further adjectives with negative connotations, such as 'different', 'wrong', 'frustrating', 'unmotivated' and 'bad'. These negative adjectives are paired with personal pronouns to make it feel like this piece is being addressed directly to you, whether you are a teenager or adult reading the piece: 'what I really hate though' and 'I am just expected to know'. These pronouns force the reader to think about these points and realise the unfair expectations the question puts on teenagers. Short sentences also hammer home the writer's negative feeling towards this question, and her attempts to answer it. For example, 'That is a very bad idea.' Coming on the heels of a series of long sentences, this short sentence highlights how she feels, that she can't answer 'the rude question' correctly no matter what she does. The author is trying to raise awareness that adults are putting too high an expectation on teenagers when in fact, as she points out with her rhetorical question, 'how many adults, at the same age, knew what they wanted to do ...?' Her message to adult readers is that they should think of something else to talk to teenagers about and to 'try putting themselves in our shoes', so that they might think twice about putting such pressure on teenagers who have not yet figured out their future plans, just like the speaker.

NON-FICTION 5: Ducks and Drakes
Pages 92–93

1–2

rhetorical question: ... who am I to impose my anthropomorphistic disgust on a perfectly natural phenomenon?; So why hadn't he fulfilled ... or even fatal attention of the others?

adjective: full, leisurely, good, great, young, small, exhausted, jostling, careless, red, normal, long, mature, dazzling, green, tired, inexperienced, deep; lost; weak; stupid; injurious; fatal; well

parallel structure: I had lost any taste for coffee. I had lost any taste for taking photos.

short sentence: 'Weak or stupid, I guess'; 'We do.'; We are not.

metaphor: a great knot of ducks; they are innocents; his part of the bonding agreement

onomatopoeia: clapped, thud

alliteration: I **d**rove home aware of my own **d**eep measure of **d**isturbance

personal pronoun: I, you, we

ISBN: 9780170XXXXXX

<table>
<tr><td>

Answers the question and **shows understanding** of what disturbed the writer
ACHIEVED

</td><td>

The author starts his account by positively describing his intentions for the afternoon with happy adjectives such as 'full', 'leisurely,' 'good' and 'great'. This feeling changes abruptly when he is disturbed by seeing 'a great knot of [male] ducks' attacking a female duck. He uses adjectives such as 'young', 'exhausted', 'small' to describe the female duck — these words emphasise her weakness in the face of the aggressive ducks, which he describes using negative adjectives like 'jostling' and 'careless'. The effect of these words emphasises how appalled he is seeing the violence of the birds against a seemingly helpless lone female. At first he is angry and he tries to stop what is happening. He puts us in the situation by the use of onomatopoeia such as 'clapped' and 'thud', which is like being shocked awake by a sudden, loud sound.

He is even more upset when, after chasing the ducks away, the female duck, frightened of him, flies into the side of a truck. She does survive, but only after this does her partner comes to her aid, 'his part of the bonding contract'. The effect of this metaphor is to give a sense of irony because a bonding contract suggests that both will support and help each other — something the partner duck did not do.

The writer reflects on what has upset him using the technique of parallel structure: 'I had lost any taste for coffee. I had lost any taste for taking photos.' This repetition of structure reminds us of what his first intentions were — to have a nice relaxing time drinking coffee and taking photos — until he is disturbed by 'nature'.

The writer recounts this event because it makes him think about the way people treat the vulnerable. For the writer, the ducks and their behaviour could be seen as a metaphor for the way men treat women, or fail to protect the vulnerable (their wives/children), but he consoles himself asking a rhetorical question, '... who am I to impose ...?', going on to say that the ducks are following nature (they are 'weak and stupid') whereas we humans have no excuse for why we treat the weak so poorly ('We are not.'). He challenges the reader to consider what 'good excuse' do people of society have in treating others badly because we cannot claim it is in our nature — like the ducks and drakes could.

</td><td>

Convincing because provides a number of details to support the key argument and explains meaning and/or effect of these examples
MERIT

</td></tr>
</table>

MERIT answer *plus* Explains author's purpose of challenging us to think about the way the vulnerable are treated in our society. Makes insightful links and shows perceptive understanding
EXCELLENCE

NON-FICTION 6: Teenagers, or Seeds?
Pages 94–95

rhetorical question: Did you feel that shiver run down your spine?; The anxiety set in?; ... are they not still moments of happiness?; Surely a sip of joy ... glass full of cynicism?

adjective: blissful, innocence, fast, fear, uninformed, black, white, more, grey, uneducated, small, new, healthy, balanced, sickly, second-hand, bad, wrong, own

repetition: Maybe they

short sentence: Teenage naivety; Small, and new into the world; Mess up, make bad choices; The anxiety set in?

metaphor: teeth set on edge; one toe out of line; the war against teenage naivety runs deeper; innocence can shelter you; We are a generation of Peter Pans; buried in responsibility, and drowned in reality; think of us teenagers as seeds

listing: fertiliser, some water and sunlight; their warnings, their naggings and complaints

alliteration: bury a seed in fertiliser, and keep it in the sunlight for too long, it may struggle to sprout; small, sickly sapling

personal pronoun: we, I, I'm, your, my, you

imperative: Mess up, make bad choices; learn; grow, and be yourself; Live your own life

ISBN: 978017O3XXXXX   PHOTOCOPYING OF THIS PAGE IS RESTRICTED UNDER LAW.

Answers the question and **shows understanding** of the author's attitude towards how people should treat teenagers
ACHIEVED

MERIT answer *plus* Explains author's purpose of challenging us to think about the way the vulnerable are treated in our society. Makes insightful links and shows perceptive understanding
EXCELLENCE

The author's attitude towards being a teenager is that although they could do with a little bit of assistance, fundamentally teenagers should be left alone to forge their own lives. She uses the repetition of 'Maybe they … Maybe they … Maybe they …' to emphasise the uncertainty and worry parents feel about whether they have done enough for their children. And she also lists the different (negative) ways parents communicate their 'fears' such as 'their warnings, their naggings and complaints'. This list is something all teenagers can recognise that their parents do when trying to get their kids to understand the need to be careful. The extended metaphor of the teenagers being compared to seeds shows us the writer's opinion that teenagers need to be given time to develop, just like seeds which don't become trees or plants overnight. The author states that a seed with 'a little bit of fertilizer … letting it grow in its own time … will become a healthy and balanced plant'. The seed is a metaphor for a teenager, and the author's message is that they need to be able to work things out themselves and have the time to do it. Another technique that hammers home this message is the short sentences such as 'Then, learn; grow, and be yourself.' **She believes that 'there are some things that are just learnt rather than taught'. This is a good thing to realise because sometimes we rely too heavily on other people, taking their advice or even letting them make decisions for us. Harris wants the reader to realise that we need to 'live our own life' and this is the imperative she leaves us with, forcing the reader to reflect on their own life and choices and if they are allowing those around them to be themselves, and if they are allowed to do the same.**

Convincing because provides a number of details and explanation (**She uses …, so again …, This is made clear …**)
MERIT